N G Stangarone

*** WWIII ***
& THE
BIG BROTHER T-SHIRT

Gold Mind Press

ISBN-10: 1983880086 ISBN-13: 978-1983880087
Printed in the United States of America

First Printing

Dedicated to
Albert Markly and David Favelli.
One provided funding for the venture
and the latter inspiration for this book.

Contents:

Chapter One:

Death of a Working Class Hero.

"True wisdom comes to each of us when we realize how little...
...we understand about life, ourselves and the world around us."

Socrates

Today, as I typed these opening words about a prophesy painted from multi-colored oils, a shadow cast by a mournful aperture brands itself onto the psyche of a new generation. And as previously happened when the sudden and unexpected loss of a legendary music icon hijacks headlines from newspapers all across the globe; we are left in the wake of a sorrowful stupor.

Perhaps it's that their untimely demise has incrementally deprived us of some reflective truth. The profound revelation that there really are so few authentic "Working Class Heros." Obviously, I'm referring to that singular standout, one who risks their fame and/or fortune to transcend the inertia of mediocrity and become a true champion of the masses. And rising against the gravitational pull of a complacent earthly horde, they become the luminescence where none had once existed before.

But back in 1980, it was John Lennon, cultural icon and the original WCH, who was struck down in his prime by an assassin's deranged fantasy. Now however, as we fast forward almost 36 years to an April spring day in 2016, the music world is confronted with the mysterious death of the "Purple Prince of Pop."

Frankly, the most prevalent sensation, at this moment, is a difficulty of comprehension or inability to consciously accept the knowledge that Prince is now lost to the ages, for all of times. This disbelief is rather pronounced because Prince and my brother John, who is about eighteen months my junior, were both born during the 58th year of the twentieth century.

In addition to that, I can still recollect with a fairly undiminished clarity, though it has been well over thirty years that have since gone when my brother, who goes by Tony, an aspiring musician at the time, raved with an uncharacteristic enthusiasm about Prince's blockbuster film, "Purple Rain."

Still, it did require viewing the movie before I could concur with the sensational media hype which had heralding Prince as the purple cloaked, guitar-wailing mini-Superman from Minnesota.

But now a cosmic emptiness intrudes my feeble sense of immortal longing. It's as though a meat cleaver of galactic proportions has disjoined our collective time line. Effectively rendering what was from what is now with a demarcation of time eternal.

But this will be as far we'll go with drawing (no pun intended) any other similarities between the deaths of these two rock music legends. And with that, please allow me to articulate the narrative thesis for this manuscript. Basically, it states that the assassination of John Lennon inspired a painting which foretold the coming of World War III.

                    *   *   *   *   *

It was genuinely peaceful and serene that frigid predawn morning in early December of 1980. Having just regained consciousness from an unintended slumber, I found myself reclining comfortably on one of a pair of blue love seats guarding the foyer of the Research Center at was located at the far southern end of the Chicago Botanic Gardens.

On duty that early morning as night watchman for the CBG, "nodding off," would have been a workplace infraction that could have exposed me to a serious reprimand. Even though the head of the security department at the Gardens, Gene Brandt was always a kind and wise manager of exceptional aptitude and would have rendered the appropriate caution or verbal reprimand.

Anyway, the sudden nap had been induced by the soothing warmth so generously provided by the heating vent directly behind the navy-blue chrome framed polyester love seat. It had been a cold, blustery evening and the vents were pumping out copious volumes of heated air. Enough to toast a pair of cosy cushions into massive tranquilizers that knocked me unconscious only minutes after taking a seat. But immediately upon having shaken my conscious mind free of any lingering traces of some forgotten dream, I quickly sprang from my rosy recline and began to earn my night's wages.

So starting with the key station conveniently located at the front entrance, I inserted the punch key into the keyhole of the watchman's clock with practiced dexterity. A loud metallic click resonated in the silent darkness, as a swift twist of the key sounded like the chamber of a rifle being loaded. And thus the time card was duly marked at approximately 3:13 am. After another clanking twist, the shaft of the punch key is pulled from the tightfitting keyhole and laid back into the little key station with another noisy clank. Releasing the leather bound watch clock from my grasp, it dangles freely at my hip from a thin black leather strap draped over my right shoulder. Determining that the coast was clear to proceed, I walked with my friend, Mr. Stealth, through the shadow ridden hallway leading to the Research Building's front office.

Opening the door to the research office, I stepped into the sightless vacuum of empty darkness. With the flick of a wall switch, a brilliant burst of light shocks my retinas with vision. Through squinted eyes, I reckoned sight of the key punch hanging from its chain at the far end wall. Casually passing the first research desk, a sudden impulse urges me to turn on the portable multi-band radio just sitting within reach.

Then, as I continued toward the beckoning punch key, the first words reproduced from the radio speaker echoed a sonic reverberation that rang through the chambers of my mind, "John Lennon was pronounced dead last night..."

First spontaneous thought was that perhaps this was a moronic attempt at spreading shock across the radio sphere. A crude homage to the 1938 "War of the Worlds" radio skit that was spontaneously orchestrated by the late great impresario, Orson Wells. Or possibly more along the lines similar to the Paul McCarthy death hoax of late sixties "hippy" era. When the rumor that Paul had died in Vietnam began to circulate across Beatleland.

But as I reached the key station, a hideous shade of tragedy colored me with the deepest stain of blue. It was a melancholic afterglow resulting from the instantaneous realization that from this moment onward, the world had irrevocably changed.

Personally, its perceived change was directly proportional to what I'd experienced as a spirited youngster witnessing the first Beatles performance on the "Ed Sullivan Show." It was way back in nineteen sixty-four, approximately sixteen years prior to that dark December night. Watching John,

Paul, George & Ringo play to pop perfection, I was consciously aware that the famous fab of four were actually within walking distance from the apartment dwelling where my family called home. And it was truly mind blowing because I had musically experienced this historic televison spectacle with the understanding that it was an authentic cutting-edge happening right here and right now in the cutting-edge center of the universe, NYC. In other words, it was a global happening par excellence with Sputnik, John Glenn's trip to space or even the JFK presidential assassination, which had happened only months prior.

But as the radio report continued, a stark reality had struck my senses raw. It was a disagreeable sensation, one I'd not encountered since 1970. And it didn't concern the Beatle's official disbandment. Instead, it was when little Johnny Latanzio, a friendly and bright first grader, (about my same age when I first watched the Beatles on Ed Sullivan), was tragically run down in front of his home by a school bus and witnessed by his grief stricken mother on that most sinister Friday the 13th. I can still recall with awful vividness how it felt like a knockout blow from a raging Tyson and when "Iron Mike" was in his devastating prime.

I knew little Johnny because his family came from the same region of southern Italy where my family had emigrated. And the wrenching vision of Little Johnny's mother wailing for her dead son at the funeral home burned an eternal stain of pain on the contours of my soul that will last me till death, if not beyond.

So when Lennon was murdered in NYC, like the billion or so people on the planet claiming to be a Beatle fan, I struggled to find some strand of logic within that horrendous heap of mindless madness. But sadly all that could be reckoned was that the dream which Lennon once alluded to was indeed, truly over.

Yet, with the celestial passage of nearly four decades, it may perhaps be possible to peer back at that tragedy with some slight sliver of eternal wisdom. From where one may state with a reasonable degree of certainty that to simply accept the assassination as the deranged act of a lone wolf is to render oneself totally ignorant of the pervasive decadence that had begun to unravel the moral framework of our modern society with an unprecedented fury of cultural degradation.

The great experiment was suddenly turning rancid with a moral decay brought about from a veritable cornucopia of vices, both modern and ancient. And unfortunately it happened far faster than the human mind was competently capable of accurately interpreting the torrential stream of daily data inputs within the revealing ramifications of their important historical context, so we accepted our collective degradation without compunction.

So I believe that to espouse the "lone wolf" theory is merely a foolish attempt to placate the simplistic notions of a grossly distracted public. And worse, it absolutely obscures any other explanations that involve other significant forms of societal intervention or malfeasance.

For example, I believe it could be argued that the barely unhindered access to firearms constitutes a passive, if not primary enabling mechanism contributing to Lennon's demise. However this may relate to an American's constitutional right to possess semi-automatic or fully automatic rifles or handguns will not be addressed in this book because it's beyond the scope of its core topic, the "Big Brother" t-shirt and how it exposes the vast chasm of societal differences between 2018 and 1981.

But also instrumental to the Lennon tragedy was the burgeoning materialistic creed of modern Americanism. Where upon, the chosen American is free to be as greedy as their capitalist hearts desire. But more than that, Americanism gives one the right to acquire whatever they might desire to possess.

And after all, it wasn't a Soviet Communist or Chinese Marxist-Leninist that struck down Lennon. It was just your typical homegrown American Capitalist. And sad to say, the assassin also happened to be approximately the same age as this author. But also, just as relevant and troubling, at least on a personal level, was that John Lennon was killed in the city of my birth! And that loathsome truth is something I find particularly painful to fathom.

Yet, what had transpired in New York City, back in 1980, should have been interpreted as the proverbial "canary in the coal mine" warning that something dreadfully lethal was afoot. Where in the far reaches of a mother-lode goldmine, the scarcity of breathable air asphyxiates the luckless yellow bird warning its master of pending doom. Here, within the wording of this manuscript, the analogy represents the lethal scarcity of common sense and virtuous wisdom that leads to the asphyxiated death of a true democracy.

I say this because I lived through these tumultuously-laden times and was much the willful participant in that highly promiscuous "decades-long" marathon of spectacular cultural debaucheries. And what took place that cold and awful December night in the tender bowels of New York City was a stupendous implosion of a cultural rebellion that had reeked of an entire generation. It encompassed the rainbow spectrum of a society's emotional angst and exhilaration that throughly gripped the progeny of a war-scarred generation. Basically, a collective psyche eternally scorched by the firestorm of a global conflagration, known historically as WWII.

The Beatle's rhythm guitarist, John Lennon was born in that war-crazed year of 1940. Just as many on the North Sea Island were bracing for a devastating collision with the world's most formidable military force. But it was with this impeccable timing, that the newborn Lennon had unwittingly managed to precede the leading cusp of an invading hoard of "Baby Boomers" yet to be birthed. And so he was perfectly placed for his role as a the global "Pied Piper" for an entire generation.

On the other hand, 1956, my birth year, was positioned within close proximity of the peak value for the bell curve of America's boomer birth rate. Other peak birth babies would be, rather sadly, Lennon's assassin and by perverse comparison, Steve Jobs and also Bill Gates. But more importantly, it was a time of peace for the United States, as the Korean War had become a military blunder to forget and the scorching flames of America's Vietnam War were still French kindling.

Also, the "baby boomers" entered the world when the United States was perceived to represent the greatest military and economic power on earth. This ascertainment was revealed in President Eisenhower's departing speech concerning the dangerous potential for America's growing military complex. Though, I suppose the Soviet Union's communist military elite and Politburo would have naturally thought otherwise.

Obviously, the fact Lennon's assassination occurred during the most festive holiday season of the year only acted to accentuate the horrific crime into a somewhat primal outpouring of global angst. This was especially true in the United States. So with college finals dancing in my head, I had to shake off the grieving and make it through to winter break; all the while hopelessly cast about by this incredible emotional whirlwind.

And then, during this tumult of celebration and grief, it came to me in a flash. It was a profound vision of such visceral intensity that it exploded the known parameters of my mind into the far reaches of revelational ecstacy. And once imagine in my mind's eye, I knew it had captured the swirling premonitions that had been reoccurring since learning of Lennon's tragic demise.

After which, almost miraculously, I felt wholly separated from the melancholy which had so firmly perplexed the haunted cavities of my soul. However, in the wake of instant relief, I was swept over by a tsunami of urgency to render the vison quest; while it shone brilliant across the fabric of my imaginative mind. And soon after began exploring the means by which I could faithfully reproduce the blinding vison on painted canvas.

Opportunity presented itself shortly thereafter, when I ran into a good friend from highschool. I fail to recollect exactly where I had crossed paths with Tom Favelli on that fateful night. But I can state with a fair degree of accuracy that it was somewhere in a Highwood tavern. And most probably, either Boomer's, Silver Dollar or the Wooded Nickel. As they happened to be three of the more popular drinking holes for the local inebriates and hell raisers.

I hadn't seen my old pal Tommy for a year or two; ever since he'd been working in the city of Chicago as a photographer's assistant and I'd been working and going to school full time. During the "get reacquainted" conversation that erupted between hardy gulps of beer, Tom mentioned his intentions to setup a darkroom to developed his own work. At the time, Tom had been working on a pet project of his; using a Polaroid camera to take instant portraits of everyone he'd met.

Back then, Polaroids were hitting their zenith with the ubiquitous SX-70 camera. While first introduced in 1947, the inventor would also personally introduced the SX-70 about a quarter century later. It would have been interesting to see whether Edwin Land's product presentation was anything like Steve Job's corporate pronouncement of the Apple iPhone another quarter century later?

Tommy's idea of collecting stranger's mug shots was intriguing, especially for a book project or even a photo show. And certainly with today's social media hyper-connected platforms, the possibilities are stratospheric compared to what was even considered practical in 1980.

But before derailing any further on a tangent, it was during this conversation that Tom had mentioned the availability of rental space at the vacant Sun Valley dairy in Highland Park. Immediately the thought of opening a studio had struck me as being optimally suited for painting the nine foot oil painting of my vision quest.

<u>

Chapter Two:
</u>

A Vision Quest Beckons.

The frigid aftermath of a January storm left everything white and lifeless. With a sharp turn of the leather bound steering wheel, the Triumph bounded onto the snowy drive leading to a complex of brick buildings once housing Highland Park's milk delivery works known then as the Sun Valley Dairy.

A sudden jolt of anticipation induced an over extended step on the accelerator, revving the wheels into losing traction. But the sideways slip only elicited a thrill, as I manually worked the shifter into second. Up ahead, about twenty yards, I noticed Tom's jeep was already parked.
 Pulling up alongside, Tom came into view as he spoke to a middle-aged man standing alongside a white pickup. The bright sunlight cut through the mist that lingered from each word spoken, as they both tried to keep warm in their heavy winter parkas. Not wanting to keep them waiting any longer in the wintry freeze, I quickly sprang out of the sports car and rushed toward them with a friendly smile.

When first introduced to Mr. Amidei, I was immediately struck by his sincerely affable disposition. He was acting caretaker for the property and suggested we go have a look at the rental space. The building housing the rental space was an imposing structure, especially as we climbed the half dozen stone steps up to the entrance door.

The very moment we entered, everything seemed to fall into place as if in a Hollywood movie, as it was perfectly suited to what I had in mind. From its high ceilings to the "robin-egg" blue doors and matching trim that framed immaculate ceramic-tiled walls of white, it all spoke graciously of it's previous occupants.

Thinking back, my first recollections of the Sun Valley Dairy, were always associated with being truly wholesome and nurturing. And though I was never fortunate enough to have toured the dairy when fully operational, walking into the studio on that cold January day reverberated with the spiritual remains of small town values and integrity.

Without sounding too sentimental, this cluster of buildings situated alongside the Chicago & Northwestern train tracks represented a cultural artifact from the quaint lakeshore town of Highland Park, as it had once been. But as with many such towns long since over developed with condominiums, apartment buildings and Mac mansions, their original uniqueness has been trampled over by the bland similarities of unfettered commercialism.

As to whether my impressions were formed simply because the product the dairy provided was milk, cannot be denied. However, this was also due to the fact that Sun Valley Dairy was owned and operated by the Santi's. And they were not only well respected in the community, but I happened to have a Santi in class all through grade school. And from personal experience, Mike was one cool kid.

Anyway, the whole complex of buildings housing Sun Valley's dairy operations, quite sadly, no longer exists. Just a few short years after Sun Valley Studios had moved out, the buildings were conspicuously replaced by a mediocre rise of nondescript condominiums, And as far as I know no visible signs of the original brick structures remain. But from what I can recall those solid red brick structures had once appeared as though they were built to last for centuries. Yet, they too fell inconsequential to the awesome sway of the greedy condo craze.

Anyway, as it was back in 1981, the space available to rent appeared to be ample enough. It was basically about a quarter of the whole building which also consisted of cold storage and bottling facilities. And as was previously mentioned, Mr. Amidei, was really accommodating from the start. He was that kind of person, who upon meeting, you could immediately trust with a handshake. And so, with just that, we had the keys to Sun Valley Studios.

Shortly after, we agreed to adopting the Sun Valley Dairy logo as a way of paying homage to the old dairy. And it was only a few days later when Tom showed up with a set of business cards featuring the simple but beautiful poignant sunrise logo once used by Sun Valley Dairy.

That same day, the plans to turn part of the studio into a darkroom had absolutely sweetened the deal and turned the decision to move a studio there look like a checkmate move. Tommy seemed all stoked because the overall floor plan with the narrow enclosure at the rear presented a highly space efficient darkroom. He was also working on plans to install some plumbing for the chemicals and rinse. And we agreed to come in one weekend and paint the darkroom with a fresh coat or two of flat black paint to cover up the "robin-egg" blue wood trim.

Soon after, my darkroom equipment was deposited in a corner of the designated darkroom. The bulk of this equipment was a Vivitar color enlarger. Which touted a new invention called the "Dioptic" Light Source as its major selling point. But basically it was a color head that produced high intensity light with virtually no heat. The power behind this light source was the "Light Pipe," a translucent rod that possessed a few undisclosed special properties for a more effective glow.

When the color enlarger was initially purchased a few years earlier, it had really consumed a good portion of my time. Fortunately a few prints from that creative effort probably help me get into the Art Institute of Chicago because over the years I had given away the majority of artwork as gifts. But of the best prints I developed from that period involved using slides I shot at a 1975 Rolling Stones' concert to create imaginary illusions of rock and roll frenzy.

When Tom moved his darkroom equipment into the space, we basically had all the equipment needed to set up a professional darkroom, though on the small side.

As part of our agreement, Tom was to use half of the remaining studio space for his studio photo shoots. And within a day or two, he was busy installing a professional backdrop for upcoming photo shoots. It was also during this period that I'd begun preparing the space chosen for the nine foot painting. It was the first corner of the large office that caught my eye that initial walk through.

This also had worked out rather remarkably. That was because basically the studio was one large rectangular space, where one end had been partitioned by a wall with it's own door. This segregated area or designated darkroom had cordoned off approximately fifteen percent of the entire length. The remaining eighty-five percent provided more than ample work space for photo shoots, painting and occasionally throwing a party or two; maybe even more.

Because from the stories I would hear from along the grapevine, there was more than artwork going on at the studio those evenings I was absent due to either work or school. Well, this carried on for at least the first few months or so because from the outset Tommy and I had agreed to share the studio with the two friends from highschool. But this was only after each had expressed an interest or willingness to study from my technique or at the very least, work on their own art pieces.

However, after leaving a note about the mess I had to deal with after one of their parties, all I got was excuses deep fried in grief. I suppose they took offence after someone came across the note and made a big power play deal out of it, though it wasn't. Anyway, shortly after that "note" incident they decided to move out of the studio. And it's quite likely that they'd decided to leave even before the note had become an issue. Anyway, the fact is there never was anything at the studio that even remotely resembling art-in-progress. The important thing was that they both left of their own accord and all was pleasantly harmonious.

Now it would be appropriate to note that while in 2018 the world is awash with a bewildering multitude of entertainment technologies for leisurely enjoyment. But back in those days, that is the late seventies, the ubiquitous form of electronic entertainment, aside from the color television set, was the high fidelity stereophonic receiver with amplifier, a pair of large cabinet speakers and either a a turntable for playing pressed albums or its counterpart, the cassette deck for playing magnetic tapes. Of course, back then that was all we thought we really needed.

So my first project, that is, after cleaning the designated area was to set up the stereo. A vintage stainless steel milk-box was recovered from the trash heap of history because it was emblazoned with the Sun Valley Dairy logo. I had immediately recognized it as an authentic artifact from those halcyon days of dairy and worthy to remain as testament to their noble endeavors.

And so its usefulness hadn't ceased as it would now carry on as a sturdy stand for the entertainment center. This included a Panasonic stereo receiver that was piggybacked by TEAC cassette player. This stereophonic combo was then wired to a pair of large DLK cabinet speakers. Of course, the speakers were strategically placed to reproduce the greatest maximum stereophonic effect within the studio's rectangular confines.

Once the tiled studio walls were pulsating with the vibrations of rhythmic syncopations from a range of popular rock melodies, either provided from my collection of cassette tapes or from Chicago radio stations like WXRT, the assembling of the massive wooden frame could be undertaken.

Since the finished painting would measure out to a commanding height of nine feet, the canvas fabric that would be stretched over a reinforced frame had to measure nearly ten feet by seven feet or about seventy square feet. A costly sum of material, especially for any college student paying their own way.

Then there was the lumber necessary to construct a frame capable of withstanding the force that would stretch the large canvas taunt enough to bounce a coin. Don't recall how I actually transported the ten foot lengths of pine to the studio, but the ludicrously audacious sight of ten-foot sections of one by twos jutting out from the sporty TR-7 must have been something comical to observe. Thank god it was long before social media and the ubiquitous smart-phone camera.

So with the stereo rocking the studio walls, the lumber was measured and miter cut to size before being laid out on the floor in the form of a large rectangular frame. Surprisingly, the increase in size did not present any additional difficulties in the frame's assembly. However, structural support from corner struts and a center bar were added to prevented any buckling or bending to the frame's rectangular shape.

After constructing the frame sturdy enough to stretch a rhino hide, the next step was to dress the stretched canvas with a shroud of fresh sweet canvas that had been expertly grown with loving care on a canvas farm, far up high in the mighty Himalayas (well, maybe not). So, after spreading the sizeable off-white canvas across the studio floor, the lumbering frame was then laid directly center of the outstretched fabric. And from there, where the frame and canvas lay, the laborious work of stretch and staple began. Basically, this entailed stapling one section of canvas and then moving to opposite side of the frame and stapling another section of canvas to form an overall tight stretch. This process is then repeated across the entire length and width of the frame.

Once the canvas was stretched taunt like a big bass drum, a primer coat of gesso produced an excellent surface for the vibrant hues soon to come. And when the primer had set, the venue of white canvas was ready to receive the vision quest burning in my head.

What random thoughts may have crossed my mind at that moment are now resistant to recall. Yet, one which should have occurred is the perplexing inquiry that lingers to this day; how in the hell had I gotten myself into this predicament? After all I was just one fan among the billions or so Beatle fans that existed across the planet. I mean, thinking back on it now, I should have been concentrating on my studies, as I was also enrolled at the UICC (University of Illinois at Circle Campus.)

Because aside from paying my way through school, it was only after a concerted effort of hard work, sweetened with a dash of luck that I had managed to reach that point. Especially since I had single-handedly (no pun intended) torpedoed my academic opportunities while in high-school.

More specifically, the fact that I was suspended twice for a total of four weeks and narrowly escaped proceedings for my expulsion from HPHS, had effectively derailed any attempt to realistically seek enrollment at any respectable college. So, besides nearly eliminating the opportunity to graduate that school year with a high school diploma, I had completely given up on the idea of seeking admission to any college or university for the following year. However, this will be as far as we shall dwell on this particular tangent because while worthy of being made into book on its own merits, it detracts from a storyline or thesis already complicated in it's own write.

So, let's get back to what was happening about the time of Lennon's assassination. As previously mentioned, I was working full time as a night watchmen at the Chicago Botanic Gardens while also attending university during the day. So the recollection of how I managed to get a job as a night watchman for the Chicago Botanic Gardens may provide some insight to what inspired the painting.

First off, I would be remiss, if I did not take this opportunity to mention the second person I encountered at the Gardens, following Ray, the CBG's trusty building engineer. That's because Ernie Terrell was truly someone like whom I'd never met before nor since. However over the passage of time I'd have to say that if anyone reminds me of Ernie, it would have to be that legendary blues musician, Son House. They both share a genuine graciousness that was easily displayed by the way they related to all people with genuine friendliness and "down to earth" charm.

Personally speaking, Ernie was always a truly humble and wise old soul from the deep south. And frankly, I hold the greatest respect and admiration for Ernie and feel fortunate to have known him in my life.

And it had nothing to do with any financial wealth or professional stature. Because frankly, Ernie was the head janitor at the Garden's Education Center. But in reality, he was the Garden's unofficial "good will" ambassador.

Anyway, suffice it to say, Ernie gave me the job. Even though, the Education Center's building engineer, Ray, was for whatever reason, hesitating to offer his acknowledgment. But thanks to Ernie, it was decided that they'd chance it on the kid from nowhere. And so in October of the year 1977, I first began working at the CBG as a janitor.

All in all, the job was not without it's benefits, for while the nastiest aspect (hands down) was cleaning the restrooms. And without exaggeration, the women had the men beat, though not in a good way, either.

On the other hand, when it came to vacuuming the carpets, especially in the museum and library, it could be rather relaxing. And after the early morning rush, there was plenty of down time, which I filled with plenty of reading.

Ernie was quick to humor and on a few occasions joked that he was the boxer by the same name. Of course I'm referring or rather Ernie was referring to the legendary WBA heavyweight champion from the middle sixties. Anyway, his affable manners meant that all sorts of people knew who he was at the Gardens. And throughout the day, they would approached Ernie just to exchange a hello. And Ernie would greet each and everyone of them with a warmth that rang true to the heart. It really seemed as if everyone loved Ernie at the Gardens.

Shortly after getting hired that mid-October of '77, a friend who will remain nameless was looking for a job. If I remember correctly, the Gardens may have been looking for another janitor to help out over the approaching holiday season. Anyway I do remember speaking to Ernie about my unemployed friend. And upon my recommendation, Ernie was generous enough to hire him for the holiday work schedule that very day.

Unfortunately, my friend wasn't the only recently hired, because about this very same time the Gardens also hired a pair of "former policemen" to run the security department. This was the result of several unprofessional antics perpetrated by the in-house security staff over just the relatively short duration of my employment.

For whatever reason, not long after my friend started working at the CBG, he began conspiring with the two security guards to orchestrate a coup of the custodial department. Basically, from what I was able to surmise, these three amigos presented the management staff with false accusations against Ernie. Grossly stating that he was negligent of his custodial duties. But this a false accusation fabricated on the pretense that they could provide the same janitorial services at a less cost than what they were currently paying Ernie and his janitorial crew.

My so called "nameless" friend had not only back stabbed me, but he had backstabbed Ernie. The man who gave him the job in the first place! And even though Ernie had hired him mostly out of a genuine compassion to help someone on the down and outs.

Honestly, I could have cared less about losing a janitor's job after less than six months. But this was Ernie's livelihood. And he was a middle-aged African-America, who had been breaking his back on menial jobs for God knows how long. Now, you tell me how in da' hell, he was just going to move on and find another job in late seventies America. And here was my young, blonde and blue eyed friend taking this man's job! What the hell is going on out here? (It's a rhetorical question, so don't bother to answer.)

In my eyes, it wasn't only pretty despicable, but I also felt partially to blame for Ernie's wrongful termination. Anyway, there was nothing I could do about it because I had also been terminated or layed off. I don't have any incriminating evidence, but I do believe it was part of the political bullshit which occasionally went down at the Gardens. Because, quite frankly, the CBG is a highly profitable non-profit entity.

It was difficult not to pity a friend, so I never confronted him about the betrayal. And as far as I'm concerned, never will. I'm not here to judge any of my friends and to forgive is something that increases in value the more it's freely given.

As fate would have it, I had been blessed with an angel at the Gardens who answered to Lucy. I believe she ran their educational department which conducted horticultural classes for visiting grade school students. She was a pleasure to meet everyday I worked there as a janitor. And I don't recall exactly how she became aware of my artistic abilities. But sometime shortly after leaving the Gardens, she asked if I would paint a wall mural in her classroom. So by March of '78, I began painting the mural. It was titled the life cycle of a seed plant and showed in a concentric series, the specific stages of a sunflower plant. Within a month or so, it had been completed with signature.

The mural was well received by everyone at the CBG and afforded fleeting status as "artist in residence." This lead to being offered other creative-orientated jobs at the Garden. And for a short while even designed window displays. But after only a week or two, maybe three, I came to the realization that it really wasn't my cup of tea and quit. But fortune smiled on me once more and by then summer employment positions were opening for landscaper and construction crews.

And again I had the good graces to join Rick's crew. Well, it was really only Rick, myself and his trusty brown truck. But Rick was a great guy. He had a college degree in forestry and was striving for a career as a Park Ranger at a national park. Don't know if he ever did, but it would have been something to have run into him when I used to make frequent visits to Yosemite National Park.

And suddenly I found myself beginning to developed a latent fondness for horticulture. But most especially, it was about developing a true appreciation for the amazing lives of trees. Though there was one other previous time when the life of trees was made apparent to me. It was in third grade. And for whatever reason, Mrs. Sesso shared with her young pupils how upsetting it was for her to see a rusty nail protruding from the trunk of a poor, defenseless tree. And to get her message across to our little fertile minds about how awful it was, she asked us, point blank, how we would like it if someone hammered a nail or two into our skinny little chicken legs. Well, she didn't use that exact term, but the thought sent an instant shudder down my spine just contemplating the intense pain. I mean, at that age, the thought of getting a needle injection would have induced a surge of angst-ridden panic.

So with sharpened pruner in hand and Rick acting as tree tutor, I attempted to master the art of pruning. Using hand shears, we basically clipped off the little green shoots that would spring up on the trunks and lower branches of the Garden's substantial selection of trees. And of which one of these many variety of trees we pruned was the gingko. And to this day, just about every time I notice the distinctive dovetail shape of a gingko leaf, I instantly recall Rick saying that until they had discovered a living specimen in China, the gingko was believed to have been an extinct species.

Also, on one particular day, Rick, being of French ancestry, as he so informed me, made an effort to reacquaint me with the French nation's celebration of "Bastille Day." Obviously, he'd made a wise choice in obtaining a degree in forestry and not history.

And well, that pretty much summed up for the first half of the summer; drive up to a tree or a grove in the pickup truck and then go to town cutting off all the green shoots we came upon.

However, for a week or two, when Rick had gone on vacation, I was assigned to the grass mowing crew. There were several of them roaming the vast grassy acreage of the CBG. That is, everyday it wasn't raining. Each morning, we would break up into rat packs, much like motorcycle gangs and repeat a circuitous route all across the vast grounds. The majority of the mowing was conducted over leisurely slopes and mundane flat lands. But occasionally I had to leap off the mower seat and push with all my strength to keep the heavy machinery from sliding down the slippery embankment of one of CBG's small islands and falling off into the murky lagoon.

But the real cool thing was that at times, like a faux motorcycle gang traveling at will, a few of us would head off to a secluded portion of the Garden's and share a marijuana joint. Then after torching up a "big fatty," riding the mower didn't feel much like work at all; more like a fun day at the park.

When my brother John came back from his summer break at SIU, he accompanied me to the garage where all of CBG's trucks and mowers were maintained. There he applied for any summer positions still available. And that very morning he was hired on to their construction crew. And as it worked out, we rarely saw each other that whole summer. Of course, we're talking about 350 acres. Though on occasion, I'd spot him with the rest of the construction crew working on some building project for the Chief. An old crusty sea captain lost ashore without even a dingy to ride the mighty waves. Though this would soon change when his crew finished crafting Chief's grey painted pontoon boat to captain on the tranquil waterways of the CBG.

Then as the approach of summer's end was just around the bend, fate struck again. One late afternoon, I was approached by the acting head of security, Reza Danish. A highly intelligent and well educated man who reminded me of Omar Sharif in Dr. Zivago. He seemed over qualified and out of place working security at the Gardens. But for the fact that he'd emigrated to America from Iran, he no doubt would have been much more ably employed as an attorney or even physician. Anyway, one day in late August, Reza informed me of a job opening working the afternoon shift and asked if I'd be interested. I was hesitant at first, because of my previous experiences with the Garden's security staff. But he convinced to join when he said I could study or do homework on the job if I were interested. That really sounded inviting as I was already planning to begin classes that fall.

Also, as previously mentioned, the atmosphere at the Gardens were always highly charged with an air of political intrigue. And for reasons I'm entirely unaware of, the reason why Reza was running the security department was because of a falling out with the "ex-cop" security and "back-stabbing" friend janitorial scheme that had originally caused my departure in the first place. During those days I was always busy, pretty much like practically everyone else my age, that it never occurred to me to pursue any further inquiry about what had soured their greedy scheme. But if I'm not mistaken it may have been something along the lines of embezzlement.

As a ironic footnote, shortly after the summer job had settled down to a daily routine. Some co-workers and myself were enjoying our lunch break under the cool shade of a Willow tree. It was really like a day in "Garden of Eden," at the CBG. Absolutely perfect weather that beckoned all of a kindred spirit to break outdoors into the freedom of a summer daze. I believe we were getting ready to share a skinny joint, when I saw my nameless friend. The notorious back-stabber, ride off on his motorcycle and straight out of the Chicago Botanic Gardens for good. I suppose that's why they say payback is a you know what. But best of all, with those three jerks gone, it was morally gratifying to see good ol' Ernie back on the job as head janitor.

Several weeks following that incident, I was hired to work security. And that in itself was a great opportunity. Especially since it meant that I would have both the time and money to go back to school. And hopefully earn a college degree in architecture or even electrical engineering.

And then, within that first year of working security, I transferred from working the afternoon shift to working the night shift. The position had become suddenly available after the two night guards had gotten so stoned that they forgot their bong in the security station-wagon.

The midnight shift worked wonderfully at the time because it allowed me to free up an entire day for attending school and taking care of business at will. And when in December of 1980, I was attending classes at the University of Illinois Circle Campus the course of my planned trajectory suddenly veered off course.

<u>Chapter Three:</u>

A Dangerous Field of Explosive Minds.

When the painting began that wintry day was in itself unextraordinary. And as I first donned my deer hunter's camouflage-overalls to wear as a painter's coveralls, the sound of trumpets blaring were noticeably inaudible. But as I raise the top of the rectangular painter's box, the excitement did suddenly mount. Glancing over its contents, which included a dozen tubes of colored pigments along with an equal number of brushes with various widths and tips, I opted for a stick of charcoal.

The fifty-four square feet of blank canvas began to call out my name with the voice of a sultry muse. She whispered into my ear, commanding me to enter its void and fill it with my imagination. Without hesitation I began projecting the vison quest upon the vacuum of a blank canvas. Then without a shadow of doubt, the journey required to travel toward completion appeared wholly apparent.

So with the charcoal stick, I sketched an overall outline of a fundamentally rotund roundness within a space constricted by a rectangular boundary. Once this quick sketch was scored, a skeletal pattern for the oil painting had begun to cast its threatening pose within the reaches of my mind.

Grabbing the largest brush in the box, a No.20 "M. Grumbacher" with its iconic white-tipped yellow handle, I began attacking the white canvas with oily dabs of colorful abandon. Working from a palate that initially consisted of van dyke brown, yellow ochre and some zinc white mixed in with a tincture of permasol green, I was ever mindful not to stray outside the delineated charcoal boundaries. And all the while shades of hue danced across the canvas-scape. But this preliminary foray into throwing color was merely a prelude. After that, I gradually concentrated my efforts on different sections of the painting to add subtle textures to the accumulating layers of visual magic.

And this improvised choreography of paint moved to a soundtrack of rock songs ranging from "Midnight Ramble" by the Rolling Stones, "Hells Bells" from ACDC to "Stranglehold" by Ted Nugent. Yet this rocking ruckus would alternatively be accompanied by a heavy rotation of Beatle classics, especially from the "Rubber Soul" album.

And of course with theses tunes rattling the walls, I often found myself in a frenzy of painting hostility. And thinking back on it now, it really was quite cathartic. Anyway the painting was intended to be my political statement or visceral representation on WWIII. So, it seemed only natural to throw some serious strokes of color on the canvas. Gathering momentum with each and every slash of the paint-laden brush. This conflagration of hue, from the sultry vibrancy of cadmium red crimson to a totally intriguing shade of manganese violet suddenly exploded across the once tranquil canvas face. All the colorful calamities of the world were being blended into a highly revealing soul scape of grave premonitions.

By the end of February, everything was up and running and totally copasetic. Tommy had installed a large professional photographer's backdrop against the wall that separated the main studio from the darkroom. However, the darkroom did remain in limbo, though both of our photo enlargers remained in storage there. Tom's black and white was sitting on the counter while my Vivatar color enlarger remained in its original box. And as it would turn out, they would be left stored exactly where first placed because the darkroom would never be built.

Meanwhile, Tommy was now bringing in aspiring models to shoot for his freelance photography business. One of the girls was the singer in a local Chicago band. Beside being naturally attractive, she was friendly and intelligent. Later that year, she would participate in the "Big Brother" shoot at Tommy's studio situated in downtown Chicago.

It was during this period that University demands and full-time work meant any "free" time that was found available for painting became absolutely cherished. But with the passing of time even that was becoming more difficult to find because word began to spread about the painting, so every once in awhile, a curious friend or acquaintance would stop for a spontaneously disrupting visit.

On one these occasions, a person or rather an acquaintance, paid an unannounced visit to see this rumor of an enormous painting. The painting was nowhere near completion, but as we stood there facing it, he began to inquire about its monetary worth. If my recall is correct, the reply I gave was that I really hadn't considered a price as it was yet an unfinished piece. He then took a moment or two to contemplate his next reply before making an offer of $5,000 for the painting when finally completed.

I shrugged it off as though he were was bluffing, but then he got serious and insisted that he was making a legitimate offer. But to this I just replied that until the painting was finished I wasn't interested in accepting any offer. Though at the time, I had nothing to base the speculation on the painting's price. But I was thinking of a price more in the range of $30,000 or possibly more. I believe he may have asked that I contact him when the painting was done, but I never followed through on the offer.

And over the course of several ensuing months, there would be other unexpected visitors. Some totally unexpected, though none more so than when my Mother showed up at the studio one spring morning with my younger brother, Tony. Still don't really know what that was all about. But I suppose she was just curious to see what I was working on for the last few months. Anyway, that was a trip to say the least.

And fortunately enough, I hadn't filled the studio with a pungent cloud of pot smoke just prior to the surprise visit. That certainly would have been an awkward moment to say the least.

Though as previously mentioned, the studio had been garnering a reputation as a party house. But I really had nothing to do with that rumor. Don't get me wrong, back then I was all for the party scene. However, the funny thing is that at one time I was beginning to feel like Robert Redford's melancholic leading man in the 1970's Hollywood blockbuster, "The Great Gatsby."

Specifically, I'm referring to the party scene when everyone, dressed in tuxes and gowns are enjoying one hell of a time. Yet ol' Gatsby, the party mansion's cordial host manages to remain aloof. This imagined resemblance could have also been precipitated by the fact that approximately a year or perhaps two years before I even had the vision quest, the great Redford himself was in Highland Park. He was filming his directorial debut masterpiece, "Ordinary People."

And during one memorable scene, where the troubled highschool teenager, played masterfully by Timothy Hutton, goes to visit his shrink for the first time. That shot put Redford and his film crew, within only a five minute walk from the old dairy and the future Sun Valley Studios.

And according to my mother, Redford had actually entered John Stevens, the ladies fashion boutique where she worked as a seamstress. Apparently, the famous Hollywood actor/director was scouting another angle from where to shoot that same particular scene.

So, though I may have wanted to join the festivities at the studio, it just wasn't possible with my schedule at the time. I never once participated in those late night parties. Yet sure enough, whenever I returned to work on the painting, there would always be some form of party residue left behind. Usually it was empty beer bottles and ashtrays filled with cigarette butts and a roach or two, however after one of those late night shindigs, a sole Styrofoam head remained as an eyewitness to the debauchery that had transpired the previous evening.

It was a plain white head, the type that was typically found on a fashion boutique store's glass counter to display a hat and scarf or some other fanciful adornment. Well, for an unknown reason, I immediately took a liking to that plain white head. But its blandness was disconcerting and just seemed to be asking for a spruce up. So after giving the head a highly colorful rainbow paint job, I stuck a large pheasant feather in it's forehead for a touch of flamboyance. It was then christened, "Major Head Case," and unofficially became the studio mascot. And even when I moved out of the studio, MHC stayed with me. Though over the span of decades, "Major Head Case," would eventually vanish without a trace into that constantly growing heap known as Mount Rubbish; the true testament to our post-modern materialistic world.

It wasn't but a few months into the project when spring-break made its annual rendezvous as a continental migration of stressed out students arrived on the sunny sands of southern shores. I refrained from joining my scholastic compatriots in their inebriated states of wild abandon and instead used that two week duration to throw some eye-bending colors at the work in progress.

But ironically, exactly one year later, after I'd dropped out of school and thus forfeited my claim as college student, I actually partook of this modern "rites of passage" festival. And like generations of Americans before me, I sought to experience the annual ritual ravaging the eastern coast of Florida, from Fort Lauderdale to Daytona beach and beyond.

Yet this trip only came about when Tommy and I decided to go marvel at the third launch of the Space Shuttle Columbia from the Kennedy Space Center, sometime about the new year. However this only offered weeks at most to design and silk screen the t-shirts for the shuttle launch.

But the overall plan was to meet up with a couple of friends living in the West Palm Beach area. Tom was in for the ride with ambitious plans of capturing a spectacular shot or two of the launch. I had hoped to seek a local street vendor or souvenir shop to sell an original Space Shuttle t-shirt that I'd designed during the winter deep freeze. The main thought behind the design was to make it readily personalized for each one of the numerous launches already planned by NASA. Not only this launch, but also for each of its new fleet of Space Shuttle orbiters

But the t-shirt plan never materialized because of the incredible horde of t-shirt hawkers literally lining the road facing the launch site. It was absolutely incredible at how many types of t-shirts were being sold for that one event. And greatly surpassed my expectations which had been based on the t-shirt businesses that operated at rock concerts from that time. And frankly it was rather disconcerting, considering I was still smarting from the abysmal loss I was eating on the "Big Brother" t-shirt failed venture. Almost immediately, it appeared economically unfeasible to pursue this particular t-shirt venture. (Especially as I was also preparing to market my new photo-illuminating display system.)

Tommy and I hitch a ride on a redeye flight straight out of Chicago O'Hare and got picked up in Miami by two high school friends, Kurt and Mike. It was about two or three in the morning and when we arrived at the gate entrance to Kennedy Space Center. We found the entrance booth eerily unmanned. It was quickly decided to park the car at the entrance gate and take a casual walk into the darkness of the surrounding grounds. Though chances did appear slim, this was very much a liberate attempt to find the launch site for a spectacular close-up view of the historic third takeoff of the Columbia Orbiter and its two man crew; Astronauts Jack Lousma and Gordon Fullerton.

However we weren't five minutes on base before we spied headlights headed our way. When the unmarked sedan pulled up and stopped, I thought we were in serious trespassing jeopardy. But the man, who appeared to be in his forties and dressed in civilian attire, was disarmingly cordial and unassuming. Obviously aware we lacked the proper credentials he informed us that we had to do an about face and head for the gate entrance. His friendly demeanor gave some of us the impression we had a slight chance to talk our way to the launch site. But the man was amicably adamant. So instead, we ended up with a free ride back to the gate for our paltry efforts.

But I can clearly remember as we first stepped onto the base and walked out into the night's cover of darkness, it was incredible surreal. I kept imaging that somehow we'd find the launch site and steal ourselves a front row seat to the fireworks. Very similar to when Tom and I scored front row seats to a Ted Nugent concert. And after doing a few snorts of coke right there in front of the stage bouncers and under the sneering gaze of that long-haired wild man wailing on his guitar with sheer reckless abandon. However, as awesome as that was, no doubt the launch of Columbia would certainly have scorched ol' Teddy's backside like burnt white toast.

Still, even though we had failed miserably in our lame attempt to garner front row seats to the third launch of Space Shuttle Columbia, about six years later, I was in a position where I could have practically walked up and touched Space Shuttle Discovery within minutes after making a spectacular landing. This was only possible because of James Brockway, a highly decent friend by way of my marketing job in Modesto, California. Through his contacts, he managed to secure press credentials for three of us at Edwards Air Force Base. For if I'm not mistaken, he was once stationed at the base.

It was a profoundly spectacular trip. Especially to have dined in the officer's mess at Edwards. Which to my surprise was made more awesome by the presence of the great one himself, Chuck Yeager. A genuine daredevil of historical proportions; first to break the sound barrier flying a Bell X-1 in 1947. It was almost shocking because we had just gone in to get a meal, when looking up from my plate I happened to notice someone who looked awfully familiar dining with a few associates at the next table. When I realized it was Chuck Yeager, he was acknowledging our presence with a gregarious smile. This prompted me to go and ask for his autograph and almost made a go for it. But the prestigious decorum and the exclusivity of access to the renowned quarters prevented me from disgracing the place by begging for an autograph.

And something else profound, at least to me, was the same carnival atmosphere on the outskirts of the landing site that I had also experience on the opposite end of the continent. It's curious now, thinking back on it, but the same exact festive spirit that I had witnessed at the tropical Florida launch in 1982 was right there on the desert salt pan called Rogers Dry Lake in 1988. Though, I do not believe the desert gathering was nearly as numerous as the enormous gathering for the third launch which local newspapers at time were estimating to exceed a million spectators. The POST, a daily serving the West Palm Beach area and dated Tues, March 23, 1982, (the day after the launch) printed a front page article titled,"Million Saw Columbia." The piece then began with, "...A record "launch fever" crowd gathered under the splendid Florida sun and watched in awe yesterday as Columbia headed into the heavens...Authorities said more than a million people jammed the Space Coast for liftoff. Personally, it was like the biggest 4th of July celebration I ever joined, but it only for lasted for half a day. And more importantly, instead of the fireworks display that night, the authorities let off the biggest rocket on the planet that morning.

And though the plans to market my Space Shuttle t-shirt would fail to even launch. It really was a thrilling excursion. For example, during one utterly spontaneous moment, a typical seventies housewife masquerading as a "shuttlehead" by first impressions, began to converse amongst ourselves at though we were previously acquainted. As it was, we were all in line awaiting our turn to order lunch at a fast food restaurant in Titusville.

By mere happenstance, the housewife/tourist had been standing immediately behind us. During the impromptu conversation this particular lady expressed her admiration for the silk screen design on the back of my t-shirt. In fact, She had liked it so much that she totally surprised me by asking for my humble autograph. And this was just after seeing my Space Shuttle t-shirt for the first time. Naturally, I obliged her request to give my thirsty ego a quenching boost.

There was also a fairly innocent romantic twist to the third Space Shuttle launch because I had the delightful fortune to encounter a lovely fair-haired girl of nineteen. From what I can recall she was one of the local residents, who'd also turned out for the state-of-the-art technological carnival that reeked of a brilliant future.

Unfortunately, this young lady and I were not afforded the time to become better acquainted because my three mates immediately pined for a swift return to West Palm Springs practically as soon as Columbia disappeared into the distant blue skies. The whole atmosphere was similiar to what can be expected following a spectacular fourth of July fireworks show; once the applause subsides everyone races to avoid the traffic jam that everyone causes upon those who lose the race.

However, something I'll never forget was sharing a glorious and heartfelt kiss as Columbia rocketed to her orbit, leaving a beautiful whitewashed plume that towered over the gawking mass of mere mortals gathered. And now after all these years of having realized the tragic fate of that most wonderful shuttle orbiter and its crew of courageous men and women, the thought of kissing that beautiful girl while Columbia flew for her only third attempt does far surpass what dream could dare to conjure.

I must have given her my phone number because a few years later, or so it seemed, she called to let me know she was getting married. Sure hope she found the happiness she surely deserved because from what I knew of her, she was one special young lady. Anyway I've manage to meander way off track, again. So, please allow me to quite literally transport us back to the painting and the year preceding.

And so there I was standing in my camouflage painting coveralls, contemplating various shading strategies for WWIII's massive canine teeth. Basically, how I could paint them to appear as if lunging from the beast's deceptively alluring crimson-drenched mouth. And so in the spring of 1981, as I dabbled away in the oily hues of a global conflagration my academic peers were letting loose with a semester's worth of pent-up sexual abandon on Florida's sun swept sandy shores. And as they contemplated how many shots of tequila to down before breakfast, I concerned myself with deciding which of the smaller brushes I would use after my monster brush had delineated the overall cone-like shape.

And while I didn't take the time to clock my efforts, I'd have to say more time was spent on each of the beast's two large canine teeth than practically any other principal segment of the painting. The amount of depth shading required to achieve the illusion of the lethal realism that I had envisioned demanded the effort. Also, the overtly sensual interior of the opened mouth required the application of at least several seductive shades of scarlet.

It's interesting to note how those same passionate hues also lent their visceral intensity to the raging conflagration of war which rises from the beast's forehead as it subliminally spells out, "WW III."

Prior to capturing the dynamic dance of the destructive flames, I found it helpful to study the dynamic action of different types of burning fires, either in real life or on film. And from these observations, I hoped to find that expressive state of uncontrollable chaos as the intense heat is unleashed to consume ever more combustible gases boiling from the putrid ocean of rotting, immoral souls.

____ **Chapter Four:**

The Colored Soles of Colored Souls.

While attending UICC in the fall of 1980, practical necessity dictated a thrice weekly departure on a southbound Chicago and Northwestern commuter train from the Highland Park station. Riding the rails to the city on the Northwestern always carried sensations that must have emanated from the unconscious realization that this mode of transportation came with history. And that it most certainly did, for on the seventh day of June in the fateful year of 1859, the Chicago and North Western Railway was officially chartered. This event may have been planned or a spur of the moment decision, since it transpired just shortly after the company had acquired the bankrupt Chicago, St. Paul and Fond du Lac Railroad. So by the time I took my first trip downtown, a hundred and twenty-one years had already past; beginning shortly prior to the Civil War and the Lincoln assassination a few momentous years after that.

But shooting the rails has always been, even from earliest memories, a wonderful and exciting activity; not merely a mode of transport. Perhaps the fondness stems from riding the NYC subway with my father and brother on our way to visit astounding New York City landmarks like Times Square, the United Nations, Empire State Building, the Statue of Liberty, NYC Public Library and Rockefeller Center. Or going to see the Macy's Thanksgiving Day Parade. We even traveled by subway to visit Coney Island and Long Island's Jones Beach. But there was also the nearby city harbor and docks, which were just as thrilling with its collection of massive cargo and passenger ships. Being able to stand on the dock just feet away from the massive bow of a full sized ship is still etched on my brain. Even though just walking the streets and boulevards of New York City was like going out to the movies to a six year old's curious mind.

Even that fateful June evening in 1965, when my Mother and her three young children took the westbound Amtrak "redeye" straight out of the constant hustle and bustle of a crowded Grand Central Station and into the desolate emptiness of a Pennsylvania or Ohio rural evening and early morning. We traveled through the night huddled together in a three seat row as though we were not unlike a miserable lot of war refugees. But still the train ride was not only comfortable sitting on those large, cushioned seats, but in a way, emotionally soothing. Though it was throughly impossible to sleep because of the anticipation. Yet, I could have been inclined to live on the rails because when we did eventually arrive at the Union Station in Chicago, there awaited our WWII Italian soldier, exactly twenty years from the end of the last great global conflagration, Uncle Paul. And also a fresh new set of realities that left one wondering what the hell just happened.

Even waiting for the powerful C&NW locomotive and its trailing passenger cars to arrive was never mundane, as trivial as that may sound. Because to suddenly distinguish out of the mist of a foggy horizon the indiscernible pinpoint headlight as it pierced the milky distance always sparked a certain thrill. Probably akin to what one of Dr. Pavlov's dogs would experience upon hearing the chime of their master's or perhaps tormentor's stimulus bell. Even when a speeding train approached and then passed without reducing speed, it was curious to ascertain the pitch bend that always occurred because of the Doppler effect. Or on other occasions to simply engage in one of Einstein's mental equations concerning relativity and particles approaching the speed of light.

On class or lecture days or doing research in the campus library during Fridays always presented a special late afternoon commute, as I would treat myself to a hot bowl of steamy clam chowder and a cold draft beer. The lounge or clubhouse at the old Chicago & Northwestern downtown terminal was like walking into a time trap, where everything has remained basically the same since the end of WWII. As a college student with limited funds, I would be surrounded by various traders and broker from the nearby exchanges. Intermingled among them were the lawyers, doctors and other professional business executives. Usually, they were distinguished by their attire of expensive looking power suits.

Finding my empty seat among those already occupied at the heavy lacquered and brassy bar, I would order my bowl and draft. Then while enjoying my fill, I would overhear tidbits of that day's travails sweetened by a lurid coating of locker room humor. Really it was just worthless banter to distract my thoughts while I primed myself for the return home.

Then on the trip back to the suburbs, if it were late fall, I would become throughly enraptured by the swirling kaleidoscope of autumnal reds, yellow and orange. Whereas the morning commute was spent reading the remains of whatever Chicago Tribune was left behind by an earlier commuter. The train ride back to the suburbs, gave me the opportunity to witness the full transition from urban concrete jungle to the heavily wooded trappings of suburbia.

It was during one of those Friday night commutes back north that a peculiar thought took a forceful bounce within my head. While observing several people exiting the train on their short walk to the parking lot. It occurred to me how a person's individual gait could be a tell that revealed an individual's emotional peculiarities.

Not as individually unique as a person's fingerprint, but still I wondered if it could reveal someone's personality quirks. I then began to ponder whether this could be reveal by some residual means. For example, the reliefs of footsteps or rather footprints that are captured when one walks on a wet pavement of freshly poured cement.

An example of what I mean is somewhat expressed in the movie, "Dead Poets Society." And it principally deals with one scene involving the character played by Robin Williams and his entourage of preppie teenage boys. They have made their way to the school's courtyard. That's when "My captain, my captain," tries coaxing his pupils out of their emotional cocoons by simply taking a walk. To inject a bit of self-deprecating humor, Williams begins impersonating their walks according to their stereo-typical roles.

Also in a 2014 Documentary titled, "Rise of Bitcoin," there is a scene where someone says he'd like to hack into the convention hall's security cameras, so he could possibly discover the inventor of the "bitcoin" by way of his or her walk.

And so one June evening, shortly after the closing of another school semester and the stars had aligned precisely with the planets, a few friends and acquaintances were invited to a painting party at the studio. And where earlier that day, I had arrived to prep it for that evening's gathering. First, it was necessary to clear the studio of any superfluous furniture to make room for not only the party guests but also a ten by ten foot canvas that would be unfurled directly center of the studio's interior.

Then, spaced directly center of the outstretched canvas square were arranged four plastic rectangular containers. Each container was previously filled to about a third or almost half with one of the four primary colors. More precisely, one plastic container held a red water-based pigment, another contained yellow. With the last two container holding either a blue or green watercolor based paint.

I believed from the onset, that to motivate average people, meaning persons not professionally or personally inclined to be an exhibitionist, to actually participate in this painting would probably depend on getting them very relaxed and uninhibited by introducing intoxicating substances, namely beer, wine, marijuana and cocaine into the party mix. But really nothing more than you'd expect at any respectable eighties party. So with a little roll and rock music to help loosen things up, I got them to the point were they were willing to place their feet in whatever primary color they felt comfortable with before taking a meandering stroll on the canvas floor.

In some way, this was an attempt to capture, in a very sublime and totally visceral way, the sub-conscious interactions of a small party of people acting as a representative sample of the "baby boomer" population. And whereby we could capture in some previously unknown way, insight of the unconscious interrelationship that heretofore could not have been realized by any other means.

But even after an hour or so of plying them with a concoction of booze and drugs, it was still necessary to provide some verbal prodding or encouragement to get the participants to move toward the center of the canvas stage. It quickly became apparent that this lack of action on their part was due to the total lack of direction on my part. Though, this had been a deliberate attempt not to influence their naturally occurring walk.

According to my recollection, the general reaction to the final outcome of the painting was tepid. And though no count was taken, it would be fair to say that the reactions varied from those who like the idea and those who frankly couldn't care less. However, one of the participants, a sweet young woman by the name of Lauren, did ask me for the painting. This surprised me because I didn't think anyone would care for the painting as it was not even properly attached to any supporting frame work. And as it was but a curious diversion than something more serious in nature. Anyway from when I began drawing, I have enjoyed giving my artwork to anyone who cared to ask and so I gladly fulfilled her request. Later that week, while I was painting, she stopped by the studio. Before I knew it we where alone within the close confines of the designated darkroom. Moments later we were making mad monkey love within the cage of our passionate desires.

Personally, I wasn't satisfied with the results of the painting and would have liked to have tried it again. But as you shall see that was not meant to be. Anyway with regard to WWIII, well that was coming along quite nicely after I had finally completed the giant cat's imposing canines.

Chapter Five

A UPC Barcode For Me And My Number.

To offer a better perspective on where we were halfway thru 1981, I've included the following five events that had occurred up to that time:

1.) The Iran hostage crisis was a diplomatic standoff between Iran and the United States. Fifty-two American diplomats and citizens were held hostage for 444 days from November 4, 1979, to **January 20, 1981.**

2.) The first DeLorean DMC-12 futuristic sports car were produced on **January 21st.** The DeLorean was only manufactured for two years when the company quickly ran into financial troubles and its founder, John DeLorean, was charged with conspiracy to smuggle cocaine.

3.) On **March 30, 1981**, President Ronald Reagan and three others were shot and wounded by John Hinckley Jr. in Washington, D.C., as they were leaving a speaking engagement at the Washington Hilton Hotel.

4.) In **April of 1981**, NASA launched the very first Space Shuttle mission. The Space Shuttle Columbia successfully carried two astronauts, Robert Crippen and John Young, into space to complete the inaugural flight of the Space Shuttle program.

5.) On **May 13th of 1981**, Pope John Paul II was shot by would-be assassin Mehment Ali Agca. The Pope survived the attack but sustained gunshot wounds to his left hand, right arm, and abdomen. The time from Lennon's assassination to the Pope's attempted assassination was a mere six months.

*   *   *   *   *

Without school to demand the lion's share of my time while off the clock at CBG, suddenly a substantial portion of time was available at my disposal to finish up with the painting. And so not long after the fourth of July festivities, the painting was all but complete. That is, except for the artist's signature.

At the first thought, I was throughly inclined to signing the painting with my unique mark or initial. It's one I had used on other artwork already, including my "Lumus III; Man On Mars" oil painting, completed in 1979. And which nowadays reminds be of the late great Prince's symbol, though mine preceded the Prince moniker by at least a decade. Basically, my insignia is formed by superimposing the "S" initial over the "N" initial and elongating the right element of the latter so that it looked like arrow pointing to the heavens.

But after consideration, this symbol seemed inadequate for the scale and historical significance of this unique painting. What I mean is that the painting was my subliminal representation of World War III. Or at least my attempt to evoke the truly overwhelming and also horrific reality that a global conflagration could inflict on the human species, if allowed to reach critical mass, figuratively speaking. And it's with that in mind that the idea of using a bar code of my social security number as my signature came to be. For this I surmised is what we will all become; just another number in a statistical sea of casualties.

Once again, why the bar code of my social security number seemed appropriate for the "WWIII" painting is because everyone will be solely identified by a number since it is the most efficient and therefore most expedient means of managing global populations.

After all, when the inventors of the modern barcode filed a patent application in 1949. They describe their "Classifying Apparatus...," as "the art of article classification...through...identifying patterns." Yet, another quarter century would pass before the first UPC scanner at a supermarket check-out counter somewhere in Ohio first scanned any sales item. In this case, the item happened to be a 10-pack of Wrigley's Juicy Fruit chewing gum.

Perhaps what may have also inspired me could have been a news story on how the United States Department of Defense requested all products procured by the U.S. military to be identified and tracked by barcode no later than September 1981. Only weeks after my signature idea and about a dozen years after the U.S. Armed Forces began to use the Social Security number as an identification number for their personnel.

However, the next event probably wasn't the reason for choosing my social security number for signing the painting. For though the numbers weren't first issued until 1935, as part of President Roosevelt's New Deal Social Security program; it would not be until after the 1990's that the number could be applied directly on someone's birth certificate. And as such one of the painting's prophesy was realized. The sole (soul) identification for billions of individuals.

But this leads us to another more modern aspect of the social security number which is identity theft and also another hallmark of WW3. And why in June of 2011, the DOD began removing the social security number from military identification cards and replacing them by a unique DOD identification number. I don't allude to anything nefarious in that act, only indicating the defensive posture needed to protect its members from undue harm. The soldiers must wear protective gear to protect their bodies, it would seem a gross oversight if they failed to protect their personal identity from being stolen or held hostage. Which brings us to the third aspect of the barcode signature.

Reading George Orwell's "1984," will acquaint you with the concept of the all knowing, all powerful "Big Brother" concept. But this was not really considered until I came up with the "Big Brother" t-shirt. Specifically, to state its core philosophy in the most basic term: "Total Control" of the total population. But more importantly, "Total Control" is absolute power. But this concept needs to be addressed in its proper context, so I'll save further rumination on the subject till further on in this book.

For now, I'll just touch on the actual mechanics to reproduce the barcode signature accurately enough on the painting surface. First, I believe I had considered developing a stencil or a mini-silk screen. Eventually, a small silk screen was produced for the job. But before making any permanent silk screen marking on the painting itself, I tested the silk screen design on an adhesive-backed paper. It worked fine, but I still harbored doubts on how the silk screen process would work on the textured surface of the oil painting. The barcode visual effect would require the individual bars or or black vertical lines to be sharp and straight or the distortions could produce a rudimentary attempt at shading. Therefore I decided to use the test print of the barcode and adhere it to the painting where I had decided to eventually secure the barcode signature on a more permanent basis.

Still, once the barcode had been applied to the lower corner of the paining, though only temporarily, the vision quest of which I had set out to attain several months before, was now cast upon my retinas, complete.

* * * * *

Today, October 9, 2016 would have been John Lennon's 76 birthday. On a personal note, my Grandfather John passed away at the age of 76. It's difficult to imagine John Lennon as frail and elderly. But by then, my grandfather had taken some heavy blows from life in general; as when his young wife passed away after giving birth to their second child. Or that due to Italy's involvement in WWII, he would not get to see his two young girls till they were teenagers. Or that he had practically lost it all, financially speaking, during the great crash of 1929.

On the other hand, if it hadn't been for the assassination, it was a sure bet, Lennon would have continued to live out what had been already a fantastic and truly wonderful life. He had both the fame and finances to overcome any of those life altering hardships such as my Grandfather had to endure, if not overcome.

There's no reason to imagine that John Lennon would not have most probably lived a life every bit sensational as Paul McCartney went on to fulfill. And who wouldn't have wanted to swap lives with Ringo. Because when you really give it some thought, that little bugger was probably the luckiest of them all.

And who can say if Lennon wouldn't have gone on and had even better aspirations. I mean, aside from running for political office, the aged but wiser Fab Four could have staged a couple of wildly anticipated Beatle reunion mega-concert. Perhaps a few global charity events to end world strife or hunger. But of course, we'll never know. Will we?

Maybe that's what the world missed since America's 200th celebration of its Independence Day, one can only imagine how Lennon may have contributed to bettering our world with his gifts of humanitarianism. Yes, there were times he did appear to have been swept away by the egotistical riptides of his undeniably astounding success.

But no doubt, had John lived, a less mournful George would also have contributed a truly positive influence on their combined philanthropic efforts.

Yet, that too was not how it came to be.

Chapter Six

Tommy's Hot Idea.

Completion of the vision quest had been realized by the later part of July. Around that time as Tom and I were viewing the finished work reclining at a slight lean against the far right corner of the studio. Eventually the discussion came round to where the painting should be put on display.

At the time, if I recall correctly, we hadn't reached anything sounding reasonable. But not long after, Tommy showed up at the studio with a flyer he'd just had printed. It was for an arts and crafts event he called, "Hot August Arts."

Hardly more than one day could have elapsed, when Tom had presented the whole affair as if it were a fait accompli. His plan to stage an arts and craft fair on vacant property located adjacent to a strip mall bordering the north end of Highwood. And in my own estimation, he'd chosen a great venue for the impromptu event.

But more important to the vision quest was that a large unpainted brick wall faced the area where the fair's vending stations were to be located. It was just the perfect fit for the mural sized oil painting. And even better, I was only responsible for was getting the painting ready for its debut. No party logistics or marketing for be me to be concerned about.

So, I made arrangements with a friend to have the painting delivered in his van. It was a beautiful August day when the painting was transported from the studio to the event grounds. Didn't want to risk damage to the painting from any forceful gust of wind not uncommon to that lakeshore area. So using a power drill, I sunk four anchors at each corner of the painting for a sturdy fit.

But just as everything appeared set for a fitting closure to several months of artistic fervor, a terrible and untimely tragedy overshadowed everything which immediately followed. And quite literally shattered to a million shards that infinitesimally-thin pleasure pane which had only so recently begun to reflect the faintest glow of glory. However, whatever anguish I had to face paled in comparison to the grievous sorrow that Tommy and his family had to endure.

As cruel fate dictates, less than days before the premiere of Tommy's "Hot August Arts," happening, his older brother David was lost to the ages in an unbelievably tragic automobile accident. He was living in California and starting a new restaurant in the bay area. Then while returning home from working late at the restaurant, something went horribly wrong. David never returned home.

Though I never had the pleasure of knowing David on a personal level, like a close friend. Still, I can clearly recall the first time I'd seen him in highschool. I was a lowly freshman and he was a cool junior. I was with some friends in the "Glass Hall," one of several hangouts where the cool students congregated between classes.

When David and another guy who I can't recall walked into the "Glass Hall" from the parking lot entrance. They were accompanied by two girls, who I also fail to recall. Anyway, they were greeted by several of their friends gathered on the other side of the hallway from us. David had long hair which gave me the impression of him that he could have passed for a rock star.

From that distance, David came off as an authentically friendly and well liked guy. He had that certain charisma that marked him off as special.

Unfortunately, never got to know him. And honestly I don't think that we ever really talked. And for whatever reason, I can't readily recall ever really seeing much of him after that. I would hear of him from time to time through the grapevine. Yet, when his younger brother Tommy began highschool a year after David graduated, I immediately took a liking to the kid because in his own individual manner, Tom possesses similar qualities. Basically, they were both genuinely compassionate people.

Anyway years after, when I had moved to California I would occasionally drive past the very same route where David's vehicle crashed and burned. And once, for no particular reason, I couldn't help but think how different things may have been if fate hadn't intertwined with its devilish deal of the death card. All I know is my bet would have been that David would have gone far if he'd been given a chance to reach the finish line.

Personally, at the time I would have understood, if Tom had opted to cancel or at least postpone "Hot August Arts." But Tom decided to go through with the event. And I certainly perceived it as that same indomitable will that demands the show must go on, even when the worst case scenario happens.

But what I'll always remember is what happened a day or so before the "Hot August Arts" event, I had gone to see where to hang the painting. And there was Tom's father, Mr. Favelli sitting with a determined posture on his riding mower to trim the grassy venue for the upcoming event. He owned the property and wanted it to look its best for his son's event. Anyway, it was a moving sight, because he radiated a stoic resonance of such grit and resilience that it has remained undeniably admirable and unforgettable.

Yet, the pain of David's tragic passing brought back to my mind the same resonant pain from Lennon's death. I had been able to squelch the anguish that evoked the vision quest, but with the completion of the painting these emotional speed bumps were returning to noticeable proportions. To alleviate the grief, I decided to take a casual drive up the winding roads of Sheridan Road heading out of Chicago that very morning of the event. It's a drive I became acquainted with on numerous excursions from suburbia to Chi-town or vice-versa. And I suppose taking those swirling turns along the lush foliage during those late summer days always drove away the pain from my mind. And bringing a new dawn of hope across the dark horizons of my mental landscape. The interesting thing about those winding roads is that they gave me the confidence to attack the steep winding roads of the mighty Sierra Mountains during the days when I would travel from the flat lands of California's central valley to the alpine shores of Lake Tahoe or the granite skyscrapers that line the picturesque valley of Yosemite. But while the mountain turns may have been similar to some extent, the destination was entirely different in all respects.

Yet, I did sense an excitement akin to driving into Yosemite Valley as I did that morning parking the Triumph in the most convenient space available at the Highwood strip mall adjacent to the outdoor venue for "Hot August Arts." And of some pertinence to the aura of that day, one of the songs that played on the way there was sung by Peter Collins, "I can feel it in the air tonight. All my life! All my life!"

When it reverberated from the stereo speakers it sent a shiver of electricity down my spine.

Stepping out of the sports car, I really didn't know what to expect. Honestly, I was thinking it was going to devolve into a large barbeque party. When one considers the amount of publicity (which was none that I'm aware of) needed to generate enough curiosity and interest to motivate enough people to attend the event and that's not even considering there wasn't sufficient lead time to get the word out. I mean, we only had about a week or two at the most from when Tommy showed me the flyer to the day of the event. But because it really had the nucleus of what could have evolved into a tremendous art, music and food event. The attendance far exceeded my expectations and "Hot August Arts," turned into a throughly splendid day; it was as though

David was smiling on us from the shining sun up above.

But aside from a truly memorable reception, the idea for the "Big Brother" t-shirt came from the "Hot August Nights," event. Everyone I spoke with that day seemed authentically impressed by the painting. But many of them were intrigued by my signature; the UPC code of my social security number at the lower corner of the painting. It seemed to have a relevance above and beyond the painting itself. It was this impression that left me with the consideration of silk screening the UPC code of my social security number on a t-shirt. And so was born the "Big Brother" t-shirt.

Chapter Seven

The Robot and the "Big Brother" T-Shirt Girl.

I may have mentioned the idea of the "Big Brother" t-shirt to someone (perhaps myself) at the first and only "Hot August Arts." cultural extravaganza. Possibly in an off-the-cuff manner, just to liven the party talk. What I know for certain is that it was only a week or two at the most following "Hot August Arts," that I began developing the "Big Brother" t-shirt project.

This was not my first t-shirt project, by 1981, I'd been silk screening t-shirts for about ten years. It was right after I returned from Long Island, New York to begin the first semester of my freshman year at Highland Park High School, when I taught myself how to cut film with precision and adhere it to a silk screen square frame with a chemical solvent. Then I had to acquaint myself with the art of using a squeegee to squeeze through just the right amount of ink to form the stencil design on paper or fabric. Even had the opportunity to silk screen shirts for Gary Sinise, the Oscar nominated Hollywood actor/director and philanthropist. Well, actually for his highschool band, "Half Day Road." I was still a freshman and Gary was David Favelli's age or a junior in highschool.

Anyway, the original concept behind the "Big Brother" t-shirt was that each t-shirt would be printed individually with a unique bar code that corresponded precisely to that person's social security number. And this was to be my social commentary on the fact that we really all are only numbers lost in a greedy capitalistic matrix that has finally reached its fully functioning state. Like it or not, that is just a fact. Though typically, there are those who believe it's the number corresponding to their estate's net worth at the time of death that indicates their real identity.

And here lies the transparent tyranny that exists within the matrix fabric of our grand illusion that wealth conquers all; a democratic society possessed of citizens with equally shared authority and responsibilities. But how does one reveal the truth hidden behind a masquerade of lies? That is, without being affected by those lies?

In Orwell's novel, "1984," the protagonist and independent thinker Winston Smith is forced to confront the tyrannical evil that feeds on the absolute power of absolute authority. Unfortunately for Winston, his freethinking was deemed criminal and subject to the harshest penalties of their grossly corrupted laws. But the important thing to realize here is that it doesn't matter whatever sinister or benign form it may choose to assume, the objective never alters; to maximize it's tyrannical grip on the working masses to ensure its continuity of their control (power).

I can truly state that even back in the year 1981, it was already evident that we were all purposely identified by our social security number for other than the stated purpose. Because most importantly, we are being tracked and monitored by those nine numbers. It lies at the essence of global modernity. And of course with all the NSA surveillance being conducted on intercepted communications we are therefore most watched by our most private thoughts and desires.

Could this not be construed as prelude to formation of the all powerful police state signified by Orwell as the "Thought Police." For it is they, who will have been granted by the state, the lethal authority to eradicate those independent thinkers or persons whose ideas are contrary to maintaining the status quo power matrix. In other words, deemed to be perpetrators of thought-crime.

However, more than anything, Big Brother is about the total and unambiguous authority to control completely. And in order to control everyone, everyday and in every way, 24/7 monitoring is required. Once you have 24/7 surveillance, you have the means to total control. It is a very simple and predicable calculation.

But this cannot happen without provocation. Protection of "material want" will supercede the right pf personal privacy. I must give up right to any form of private existence so the rich can be as rich as they greedily can. A billionaire has more right to their billions and billions of dollars, than I have of taking a shower without public scrutiny. The rich would rather have the rest of us under constant surveillance so we could never ever pose a threat to their materialistic abundance. Because in their greedy, hypocrite minds all that we really concern ourselves with is how we can get our greedy share of their greedy lot.

But that's as far as I'll go on this conspiratorial diatribe. Now getting back to the concept of the "Big Brother" t-Shirt. The point here was that every t-shirt would be as unique as an individual's social security number. To do this required having a different bar code for each digit. So let's take a moment to examine what that entails.

First, there are an (x) amount of numerical digits for each social security number. Each digit has a value ranging from 0-9, so I had to represent each of the nine numbers with bars of incremental widths that corresponded to each numerical value.

Thinking back, and hindsight is always twenty twenty, it would seem to be that if I'd taken the time to create a silk screen for each bar and then registered the silk screen frame on the t-shirt, it may have saved some of the total expenses. But that's not what I choose to do at the time.

You see, ever since I had a silver metal-flake "skull" design heat transferred on my blue jean jacket when I visited the 1974-75 Chicago Auto Show at the Merchandise Mart, I've been intrigued by that method of silk screen because it saved on having to buy expensive t-shirts (one must consider that this was prior to the age of Walmart), so unless you could afford to buy in bulk, a single t-shirt cost at least five dollars on average. Whereas, printed transfers sheets cost only fractions of that amount.

So getting back to printing the UPC code of a social security number on a t-shirt in 1981. It may have been possible to airbrush a cut out stencil of each barcode. But it never was really considered a viable option, because my expertise was in silk screening. Obviously, I could have designed a generic bar code based on a basic numerical succession from zero to nine But in my opinion that would have just made the t-shirt just another novelty and also seriously undermine its political significance or credibility.

Therefore to create a unique barcode for each t-shirt would require a properly prepared silk screen frame for each. And that certainly could have been accomplished, either by film stencil or using photo-emulsion stencil. But the reason I couldn't choose this route is because it would defeat the very purpose of making a silk screen frame, which I believe is to produce multiple printings of the same image.

But ultimately it was determined too difficulty to register each bar and number accurately enough to prevent misprinting errors from destroying valuable t-shirt product in the process. So the obvious solution was to create decals of each bar and corresponding number.

So now I had a choice of either silk screening the decals on the transfer sheets myself or having an company print up the decals. Being that at the time I had harbored unsubstantiated expectations that thousands of people would or could possibly order the "Big Brother" t-shirt. It therefore, seemed more economically feasible to have a company experienced in silk screen decals handle the job.

But before I could make any calls I had to reproduce on paper what bar types were required and their exact proportions. Without ready access to any literature whatsoever on the UPC barcode, it was beneficial to examine barcodes already in use for retail merchandise. Then considering the practical dimensions of the space available on a t-shirt, it was easy to deduce the different sizes for each of the various bar strips required to reproduce an authentic looking UPC. Then with the help of a draftboard, I laid out the specific dimensions of each barcode to be stenciled as an iron-on decal on vellum. Cannot recall the amount of time that was required to produce the drawings, but I quickly proceeded to the next step which was to peruse my thick and trusty Chicago Yellow Pages directory.

Again things get rather foggy here because I can't recall the number of companies I may have contacted. However, I do recall rather fondly when I did eventually meet with Mr. Siegel at the Midwest Decalcomania Company. Which I found located in a large and imposing brick manufacturing plant or warehouse near downtown Chicago. The first impression I can recollect is an aura of being well established. More importantly, they were quick to grasp what I was trying to accomplish. Therefore it didn't take long for them to up come with what seemed a very fair quotation. With deadlines ticking down, I accepted the bid.

Once the means to produce the barcode and by proxy the "Big Brother" t-shirt was secured, it was on to the next step. At the time I really thought the "Big Brother" t-shirt had a message that could resonate across the nation. I needed to get the message out there, so it became necessary to advertise in a nationally distributed magazine. And preferably a monthly that could boast a large circulation.

The two magazines that seemed most appropriate at the time was Playboy and Rolling Stone. This decision was based mainly on previously issued editions from both publications. Taken into consideration at the time were just how many t-shirts and other similar novelty companies advertized in their page advertising and classifieds. Also considered was that since the "Big Brother" t-shirt ad was not only going to present a commercial offer but also an attempt to communicate a satirically political message. It was basically social commentary wrapped up in the guise of product appeal.

In the end, I did consider to try Playboy's "T-shirt of the Month," as a launching pad. But eventually, the decision to advertise in Rolling Stone was taken because it was more youth orientated. Also, provocatively speaking, more avant garde. It was sex, drugs, rock and roll. While Playboy came off as a dry martini or bourbon on the rocks with a pair of amply endowed breasts. Which is not a bad thing, but it was the status quo and the "Big Brother" t-shirt was a satirical political statement. So, with that it was decided to advertize the t-shirt in Rolling Stone magazine.

According to Rolling Stone's classified advertising rate card for the cover date 6/25/81, it cost about $2.95 per word. But camera-ready artwork including typeset meant I had to opt for their illustrated classifieds. There the general cost at the time was about $205 per column inch.

Now I just needed to create an ad. That required artwork, ad copy and estimating what costs to charge for the product and shipping. But first I needed a concept or theme that could encapsulate the overall message I'm attempting to communicate with the "Big Brother" t-shirt. Right off, one thinks of Orwell's "1984." And which back in 1981 was still the future, though not too distant. But still future it was.

Plus it was going to be used during the holidays, most especially the Christmas season. So I wanted to create the illusion of a futuristic christmas tree. For that sort of effect, I was thinking dynamic illumination or spinning, whirling christmas lights. While in grade school, my father purchased a Christmas tree stand that was motorized to rotate. I believe we may have used it for a couple of Christmas tree displays. After that it became a relic of Christmas past and was stored away with all the other relics like the spinning colored lights display and boxes of unused tinsel. Anyway I was thinking of how the Jedi Starfighter would leave a light trail when reaching light speed. By having the Christmas tree spinning with its Christmas lights on during a timed exposure, that effect in the form of a Christmas tree could be photographed.

The robot was also inspired from the Star Wars movie because when I saw the trash can at work, I immediately thought of R2D2. So now I had the background and foreground props for the shoot. Now I thought of that beautiful blonde model, Tom had brought in for a shoot several months earlier. When I told her about the ad layout and placing the ad in Rolling Stone magazine, she seemed really keen on the idea. And agreed without hesitation to be in on the shoot.

Shortly after that, Tom scheduled a shoot for the "Big Brother" t-shirt ad at his boss' professional photographers studio situated in downtown Chicago. So one evening, Tom, the model and myself hauled ourselves down to the city along with all the props.

At the studio, which was spacious and faced by floor to ceiling glass windows, we quickly moved to set up the spinning Christmas tree for the background prop, Then I quickly set up the robot in his
spot at the front of the shot.

All the while, Tom had been setting up the cameras, lights and reflectors. Then after doing a couple of test shots, we were ready to take the money shot. But suddenly, for whatever reason, our model felt uncomfortable with doing the shoot. I didn't really delve into what was troubling her because of the time deadline and frankly I couldn't afford to pay her. Anyway, it was originally a two person shot and the robot. We were going to make a champagne toast for Christmas while both of us were wearing "Big Brother" t-shirts. When she decided to pull out of the shot, it only seemed natural that I should make the Christmas toast with my robot. And so that's what we did and then left the studio as quickly as we came.

Now that we had the photography wrapped up, I just needed to finish the copy for the ad and also airbrush "Seasons Greetings," for the title that would headline the ad. Finally to put the ad together, that is the photography, the graphics and the copy text in camera ready paste-up form before submitting to Rolling Stone magazine, well, what can I say but that's where Tom's expertise really helped out. In the final analysis, Tom was very instrumental in the ad's development. And if the t-shirt would have taken off I would have taken great pleasure in seeing Tom receive monetary compensation. But as it was a financial failure, I will always be indebted to him.

*   *   *   *   *

Finally for a better understanding as to how and why the ad was developed, the following entry from my business journal dated 10/81, may offer a clue or two.

Journal Entry Dated: 10/27/81

Since I last wrote in this book, tremendous developments have transpired. I will be appearing in a national publication withing fifteen days of today for big brother T-shirt ad #1. This product contains the potential to blossom into a fad. But it is very hard to tell if it's potential has a minimal probability to succeed, all because the variables involved are many and they also have the ability to act in opposite forces for and against. I will now try to specify these variable(s).
1.) Using Rolling Stone mag.
2.) Using a Christmas theme ad
3.) Using Christmas theme ad during the last two weeks of Nov.
4.) Using a 4x4 ad instead of 2x4
5.) Using a T-shirt for a winter ad.
6.) Selling the item at the highest price $12.99
7.) Going mail order in distribution

8.) The socioeconomic environment that exists today.
9.) The Big Brother name
10.) The Ad
11.) Using a male model (dark hair, moustache.)
12.) Very happy mood.
13.) Christmas tree with spinning lights
14.) Robot
15.) Pouring a alcoholic beverage into a glass held by the robot.
**Big Brother T-Shirt*
(New Page)
16.) Using Season's Greetings as the Copy Title
17.) Having mispelled Season's Greeting
18.) Using futuristic Type
19.) Copy
20.) Using UPC
21.) Using social security.

BIG QUESTION

ARE PEOPLE READY FOR THIS?

WILL THEY ACCEPT AS A REVEALING JOKE?

OR WILL THEY SHUN IT'S SYMBOLIC
MEANINGS?

Due to the recent developments.?

future shock?

*   *   *   *   *

So by the middle of October 1981, the decals were designed and ready to be produced. Also the ad space was scheduled and the ad was shot and camera ready for printing.

The costs* at that stage were as follows:

      ★Rolling Stone Ad.................$1,240.00

      ★Barcode Decals..................$1,500.00

      ★Ad Layout...........................$156.00

*Missing was the cost for t-shirts. Since each t-shirt was printed individually it was deemed unpractical to purchase the t-shirts in bulk because of the purchase costs and storage considerations.

Basically, it was this tally of sorts which confronted me with the realization that to run the ad, outside financing would need to be secured. So with costs in hand, I contacted my accountant with my capital dilemma. But honestly, he was more than an accountant handling my taxes, he was someone who I held in high esteem even before acting in that professional capacity. I'd known Mr. Tufo for about ten years prior since he was the father of a good friend since eight grade.

There were two things that come to mind when I think of Mr. Richard Tufo. First, and foremost, what that set him apart from the other parents at that time was that he spoke directly to us, as though we were adults or he was one of us. This enamored me with an immediate sense of respect for the man. The other aspect, something that did not occur to me till decades later. It's rather odd, but I think speaks of his intelligence. Specifically, when I recall talking to Mr. Tufo by phone, there rings a similarity to what President Nixon sounded like while being taped on the Oval Office recorder. It was that rapid clip that had a cadence akin to machine gun bursts.

Around 1979, when I had formed a company called LDC to manufacture and market a patented invention of mine, Mr. Tufo was kind and generous enough to provide his accounting expertise. So it was natural to seek his guidance in this endeavor. I honestly didn't think he'd be interested in the project, but when I told him, he was not only willing to help put the financials together, but more importantly, he'd put me in touch with one of his accounting clients as a potential investor.

Still, I honestly did not believe I'd get any backers for the idea. And so I wasn't actively pursuing financing from outside investors. But at that time something about the Big Brother t-shirt concept was striking a cord, regardless of how tenuous it may have actually been. So with a tinge of apathy from a lack of anticipation, I drove out to this eclectic shop of collectibles. In my memory, it was a beautiful fall day, as I drove up and parallel parked in front of "The Ram."

My initial entrance into his retail establishment offered an impression of an intriguing mix of antique and novelty memorabilia. On his oversized business card, it describes the store as a boutique of antiques, custom clothes and jewelry. And from what I could observe it was exactly that and more so because the proprietor appeared a character right out of spy novel or mystery thriller.

Well, at the very least I could easily have mistaken Mr. Albert Markley for one of my professors at UICC. But he was really quite congenial and welcoming. By all appearance, he was fully aware of the business proposition and very keen to the "Big Brother" t-shirt concept. He immediately offered to fund the full amount I was seeking or three grand at very reasonable terms. Honestly, the whole encounter lasted no more than hour at the most and I cannot ever recall attending a more pleasurable business meeting. In many ways it was almost dreamlike. But then again, dreams can quickly dissipate in the stark light of day.

So now with the financing secured in hand, it was all a matter of going through the motions. Honestly, at the time it all seemed just too easy. And perhaps I should have taken

the ominous assassination of another world leader with more forethought. That is, as to the many ways a good thing can suddenly take a tragic turn. For it was also a week or so before the meeting that peace activist and Egyptian President, Anwar Sadat would be tragically assassinated attending a victory parade in
Cairo.

*   *   *   *   *

Journal Entry Dated: 10/30/81

Took a walk around the Sears Tower this afternoon. I was wearing a Big Brother Jersey. There seemed to be interest in the crowd but nothing profound.

12 more days
~~ / ~ / ~~

*   *   *   *   *

The Response.

There was ample room to produce the "Big Brother" t-shirts at Sun Valley Studios. Unfortunately, there were always people milling about and that made it impossible to store anything securely. Also to actually assemble the UPC barcode decals on a transfer sheet required proprietary knowledge that I wasn't inclined to share with the pubic at the time. So the transfer sheet assembly line was set up in my parent's basement. Because first and foremost it offered the privacy necessary to learn how to actually set up the UPC barcodes and then iron them on with the precision necessary to pull off the artistic illusion.

But without enough orders to justify buying t-shirts in bulk, they were purchased retail. They were manufactured by "Fruit of the Loom" and came in packages of three. At least I was starting off with quality.

To advertize with a Chicago zipcode required a half hour drive down to the city and a post office box on Clark Street, not far from Wrigley Fields and those lovable losers, the Cubs. One day, after driving down Sheridan Road with mounting anticipation, I walked into the constantly busy post office and straight toward the mailbox with key in hand. Turning the lock open with a twist of my wrist, I open the lockbox door numbered seven-eight-nine and to my welcomed surprise found it holding envelopes bearing orders for the "Big Brother" t-shirt. Though I don't believe there were more than a half dozen envelopes, it was a kind of out of body experience, to see the letters addressed to my advertized address that were sent from perfect strangers and best of all, holding checks. But this euphoria was quickly evaporated by the sudden need to begin assembling the unique iron-ons for each social security number.

The most important question of assembling each unique UPC barcode with their corresponding numerical digits was how to perfect a method that consistently resulted in an exact fitting of all the different bar elements for each individual "Big Brother" t-shirt. After considering how the social security number consists of nine digits, I calculated that this would require a minimum of twenty individual elements that had to fit to exacting tolerances within a tightfitting rectangular perimeter.

So step by step, the assembly of one "Big Brother" UPC barcode required taping one (relatively transparent) heat transfer sheet or tracing paper to a large grid pattern (already taped) to a drafting table. Then, using a Lectro-Stik waxer for copy paste-boards, I laid a thin strip of hot wax horizontally across the top portion of the designated rectangular perimeter. This was immediately followed by running the handheld waxer along the lower portion of the rectangle.

All of the different bar sizes would be pre-cut from the manufacturer's roll and placed within reach. Using the grid pattern, I would align the first bar sequence with previously placed markings indicating the overall pattern.

Now, the first bar pattern I affixed to the wax adhesive did not indicate a numerical value, instead it was meant to signify the start of the bar code number system. It was therefore specifically drawn slightly longer than the number bars to extend toward the bottom of the overall pattern. Whereas the number bars were shortened to end directly above their corresponding numbers.

So with the initial bar in place I would then fix the first number bar in place. This required both ends of the decal strip to be pressed firmly onto the two wax strips stretching diagonally across the transfer sheet. The distances between each strip remained evenly spaced with the use of a grid pattern directly behind the transparent transfer sheet. The grid pattern allowed for precision and once the bars were secured to the backing by the wax they were ready for adhesion to the t-shirt.

Which brings us to how the heat transfers were printed on the t-shirts. This was accomplished by using a professional press used for suits and other large garments. It took a couple of tries to get it right. But after that is went like clockwork. And while there was some slight waxy residue left on the t-shirt, all traces disappeared completely after first washing.

So after that first batch of orders were sent out, I began work on another batch of orders. Unfortunately, even though I had everything in place for a substantial response to the Rolling Stone ad, the number of people that ultimately ordered a "Big Brother t-shirt" was insignificant and certainly not nearly enough to even begin covering expenses.

But as can be seen by a few of the orders that were received, they came from all across the continental United States:

1.) Santa Barbara, CA (Postmarked 12/7/81)
2.) Tampa, FL (Postmarked 12/3/81)
3.) Philadelphia, PA (Postmarked 11/25/81)
4.) Madisonville, KY (Postmarked 11/27/81)
5.) North Tonawanda, NY (Postmarked 11/16/81)
6.) Shelby, IA (Postmarked 11/20/81)
7.) Dallas, TX (Postmarked 11/12/81)
8.) New Iberia, LA (Postmarked 11/25/81)

* * * * *

The Dream Is Over.

Back then, at that time I was severely disappointed by the mediocre number of orders for the "Big Brother" t-shirt. I mean it was a real kick in the pants financially speaking. But now in retrospect, it's amazing to me that anyone at all should have responded to the "Big Brother" t-shirt ad placed in Rolling Stone. I suppose, if anything, this really says a lot about those times, way back in 1981. What I mean, is that even as kids in school, we wouldn't think twice about comparing the numerical differences of our individual social security numbers for whatever childish game we might devise. You know, it was perceived no more threatening than a license plate number. It seemed so benign back then, before the coming malignancies of identity theft.

Anyway, while I had hoped to generate enough sales to cover the costs of the venture. I never anticipated generating huge profits from this endeavor because it was always really more of a personal attempt at social commentary than an actual business venture. And when one really thinks about how things could have gone horribly wrong. Even possibly exposing me to mounting legal jeopardy and expensive lawsuits. The "Big Brother" t-shirt venture harbored the potentiality to become a major disater of catastrophic proportions. Well, at least, on a personal note.

But the most intriguing as well as socially revealing thing about the "Big Brother" t-shirt venture was that no one said, "Hey, that's a crazy or bad idea," or even a simple and succinct, "Really?"

Which is something I would have been keen to acknowledge and would have taken it into consideration. Though it is difficult to say whether it would have harbored any consequence in my ultimate decision to press forward with the venture. But it's not my intention to deflect blame from this financial mishap. For I do now and have always accepted full responsibility for the financial failure of the "Big Brother" t-shirt venture.

It's just that, well, could you imagine someone proposing The "Big Brother" t-shirt today? Especially with the astounding amount of identities thefts being perpetrated today. Well, for example, if I had been possessed of an unscrupulous and criminal mind, what would have prevented me from using the social security numbers sent me and do what every other thief does with someone else's social security numbers. Of course, that wasn't the case and could never be because I have personally destroyed all the numbers that were sent for a Big Brother t-shirt.

But still, it gives me chills to think that I could have suggested that people send me their social security numbers. And the truth is I still had those numbers until just a short while ago, when I made sure all the social security numbers were destroyed beyond discernment. And I'm so relieved that I never allowed those social security numbers to be made available for anything other that what they were originally intended for, namely printing the UPC barcode.

But that's the point I'm making here, people simply did not think about those things back then. Though there was an article printed in the American Business, titled "Fake S.S. Cards Costing Billions," it was the first time I'd ever encountered the thought in public. And no doubt, rather ironic, since this article appeared the same month as the "Big Brother" t-shirt ad in Rolling Stone.

*　*　*　*　*

The Financial Fallout.

Unfortunately, back in the winter of '81, there wasn't much the time to reflect on the outcome of the Rolling Stone ad because I still owed three grand to Mr. Markley. And this was made especially so as soon as it became clear that there wouldn't be sufficient sales revenue to cover the start-up costs. And though I was employed with a full-time job, at the time I also happened to be paying my own way through college. Obviously, the first few months of 1982 would prove to be a difficult period as I searched for ways to pay back the three thousand dollar promissory note.

Fortunately, the best aspect of the deal turned out to be the fact that Mr. Markley's was a genuinely decent human being and really quite reasonable. His generosity and understanding eventually relieved me of a financial burden beyond my capacity to fathom.

However, this sense of relief had come too late as my college studies had been greatly affected by the inordinate amount of time I'd spent on getting myself into a heap financial trouble. I was forced to drop out as a direct result of the "Big Brother" t-shirt venture's abysmal failure.

Consequently, because of the financial shortfall incurred, I was also obligated to leave Sun Valley Studios. Ironically, it one year after John Lennon was killed. And my last night there I played several of John Lennon's songs on the stereo.

One those songs just happened to be his ode to all the rebels of the world, "Working Class Hero."

And as the following words played out on the stereo speakers, the truth of it all shone through the asphyxiating grief and anxiety:

"Keep you doped with religion, sex and tv.
And you think you're so clever and classless and free.
But you're still fucking peasants as far as I can see."

The nine by six foot oil painting, "WWIII," was subsequently place in storage. In 1985, the painting was dismantled. The canvas was detached from its wooden frame and rolled up like some oriental carpet before wrapped away in orange tarp. The wood frame was broken apart and discarded. Less than a year later the rolled up painting was transported to the state of California.

In 1996, the painting was unfurled but never set to frame. About six weeks later it was to be rolled up and stored away. And so it has remained hidden from world view up to this day. Though it has traveled cross-country on at least four separate occasions.

As a business venture, the "Big Brother" t-shirt was a complete failure. So much so that it still haunts me to this day. However, as a form of social commentary, I believe that the "Big Brother" t-shirt has yet to be truly appreciated. And that's because it does act a demarcation line between the happy days of post-WWII America and the manifestation of a "1984" existence.

The oil painting, "WWIII," is only now being proven visionary in its artistic scope of prophesy. Unfortunately, the prophesy the painting foretells is one that holds great consequence for all the inhabitants of this planet, Earth.

In the next chapter I hope to equate the true sense of urgency by connecting the dots between today in 2018 and back then in 1981. Pardon my figure of speech but hopefully it may alert the frog that the soothing warm waters are about to boil.

Chapter Eight:

The Watchtower Is Burning Down.

"For we cannot talk falsely now...
The hour is getting late."
Bob Dylan, "All Along The Watchtower."

The preceding chapter closed with the financial consequences of one man's meager attempt to offer some slight glint into tomorrow's fiery caldron. You know, that flash of inspiration when peering into the future's molten flux just as it flows into the ever present before instantaneously cooling into the smoldering remains of yesterday. But even if it failed to translate back in 1981, this would not preclude the possibility of sparking off some other brilliant insightful at a time yet unknown.

You see, back in 1981, the future appeared arc light bright and as a result an entire generation resorted to donning shades of complacency. That's why even after the cold blooded murder of a former Beatle on the streets of New York City, the dance clubs continued to flourished with a decadent frenzy. And everyone was bedazzled beyond their wits. How could someone contemplate it's dire portend?

There was too much money to be hustled and not enough time to hustle it all. So why worry? Be happy!

So during this prosperous period, I somehow thought I could shine a beacon of insight across the distant horizon of time by reflecting rays of light on approaching ships of doom. And sure it seems that I had proved incapable of communicating the "Big Brother" t-shirt's true meaning or that of the "WWIII" painting. Yet, to this day, there still lingers a troubling question in my brain. A thought that may possibly provide some startling revelation bearing an authentic truth to what beguiles the world today. And that question is quite simply.

Why was there not at least one solitary person who uttered but the faintest whisper of caution? If not just stating out loud how ridiculously insane it was to print your social security number on a t-shirt for the public to observe? And I'm not only referring to family or friends in my age group. More specifically those individuals in their early twenties or younger. Because I had discussed the "Big Brother" t-shirt venture with several people, who were not only middle-aged professionals, but also quite successful.

First off, there was Mr. Tufo, not only was this gentleman the father of a good friend. He was a highly competent accountant, who's clientele included numerous wealthy businessmen across the North Shore suburbs. As my accountant for my other business venture, he always presented a highly practical if not overly cautious perspective. In fact, he would urge caution to the point of discouragement when discussing marketing an invention that I'd spent considerable time and money to secure two U.S. patents.

So after presenting the concept of the "Big Brother" t-shirt to Mr. Tufo, I was surprised when he didn't offer any advice to abandon the project. On the contrary, he immediately suggested that he may have a financial backer for the project. It seemed rather surreal that on the initial presentation there was already financing available. But Mr.

Tufo set up a meeting with the prospective investor at one of his stores.

And so it was on that beautiful fall afternoon that I took that fateful drive down the winding ways of Sheridan Road to visit Mr. Markley at his Wilmette establishment, The Ram. Walking into the store was like stepping into an eclectic theater of antiques and retail novelties. Mr. Markely was gregarious with a gracious demeanor. He was obviously highly intelligent and I regret never asking him why he seemed so interested in the "Big Brother" t-shirt. But at the time I was so elated, I dared not risk offending him in any manner.

And not just for the fact that he was financing the venture with a promissory note, but that he came off as a genuinely decent fellow. But as a late middle aged proprietor of a successful retail establishment, it would stand to reason that he would have been quite wary of openly flaunting your social security number. But he never communicated the slightest bit of apprehension to the venture. Certainly, given his age and position, I would have heeded his advice as coming not only from an investor but also as a mentor.

Another individual, who may have offered some valuable insight was a Mr. Siegel at the Midwest Decalcomania Company. Located in an industrial warehouse on West Washington Boulevard in Chicago, it was a fairly large business operation with the capacity to handle odd-ball jobs like the "Big Brother" t-shirt UPC barcode. I believe at the time I was impressed by the wide variety of decals or iron-ons that Midwest Decalcomania had previously produced for its national clientele. So from that standpoint, I honestly don't believe the company needed my small order. I didn't see any reason why they couldn't have just as easily declined the job if they harbored any doubts about it's legitimacy. I would certainly think that if the concept had struck Mr. Siegel as nefarious or subject to legal jeopardy, he have simply quoted costs that would have been financially unfeasible.

Even so, there was one other individual, who's professional opinion I had also sought prior to launching the venture. And the integrity of his consul I held above reproach and whom I believe would not have been swayed by a profit motive.

And that man was my patent attorney, Mr. Parkhurst from the prestigious law firm of Trexler, Bushnell and Wolters. Their offices were located at 141 West Jackson Blvd, in downtown Chicago. From our first meeting about two years earlier, he'd always been highly informative and helpful while preparing a few design patents for my illuminated photo-display frames. Naturally, Mr. Parkhurst provided the legal consultation about the copyright status of the "Big Brother" t-shirt concept. His written reply offered no apparent concern with the conspicuous display of someone's social security number printed black on a white t-shirt.

So how is it that neither of these highly professional individuals ever once even offered the suggestion that this may be legally problematic with unknown repercussions. Please don't misinterpret or misconstrue my intentions here, for I do not wish to deflect blame onto anyone other that myself. Neither do I look to share blame on the financial fiasco that resulted from the venture. I will always accept full responsibility for the decision to market the "Big Brother" t-shirt. I'm simply attempting to demonstrate how vastly divergent were the popular views that were held and expressed back in 1981. Specifically, the concept of identity theft was not of the common vernacular at that time.

Sure, there was that article titled, "Fake S.S. Cards Costing Billions," in the periodical, "American Business." But it was from the Nov. 1981 issue, months after late August, when the "Big Brother" t-shirt concept took hold of me. Written by Gregory Gordan, it stated, "Social Security cards-dubbed "the keys to the kingdom" by investigators-commonly are counterfeited or stolen for use by illegal aliens to get jobs and collect unearned benefits."

And in the very next paragraph it states, "The General Accounting Office estimates the scandal costs taxpayers over $15 billion a year in government benefits..."

Now granted, fifteen billion dollars in 1981 was a considerable sum, indeed. And according to a fairly recent CNBC.com article dated Feb. 1st, 2017 and titled, "Identity theft, fraud cost consumers more than $16 billion." It states, "Some 15.4 million consumers were victims of identity theft or fraud last year, according to a new report from Javelin Strategy & Research. That's up 16 percent from 2015, and the highest figure recorded since the firm began tracking fraud instances in 2004."

From here, losses would appear to be fairly similar. But there are two important differences. First, in 1981 it was taxpayers that were on the hook for the losses. While today they are incurred by consumers. At face value that would appear to be two sides to the same coin. And in many ways it is, with the exception that many of the fraudulent acts were perpetrated by the citizens themselves because of the "loose distribution" of cards. It was based on the government's estimation of fraudulent claims for government benefits which are taxpayer supported and theoretically infinite. The report from JS&R estimates losses incurred directly by the consumer, who must rely on their individual financial net worth.

Also the losses in 1981 were the result of "hard-copy" issues because of lax procedures for maintaining the actual social security cards and inadequate computer software and hardware for tracking their use or misuse. That meant that if you had in your possession an authentic social security card, you could use it to get a job and it would probably never be traced. That is virtually impossible with today's digital infrastructure.

When you really think about the "Big Brother" t-shirt in today's cultural milieu, it comes off as the craziest idea. You could even say potentially criminal. But why is that? What accounts for this grand chasm of change that separates the early part of the 21st century form the twentieth century's final quarter stretch?

Obviously, back then in the late nineteen-seventies, the digital revolution could only be imagined by a few revolutionary thinkers. And it would be at least another decade before its consequences would begin to alter day to day activities. The (ARPAnet or internet) was nothing more than another tool to assist in academic research for military and scientific purposes. It was basically a multi-campus computer network, slightly similar to a high-tech hyperlinked library card file.

IBM would release it first personal computer (IBM 5150) in August 1981 or about the exact same time that I got the inspiration for the "Big Brother" t-shirt. And Steve Jobs' Apple computers were definitely useful, but comparatively speaking, the price was a bit on the expensive side. So with the world and everything in it moving in snail-mail time, it would take hours and even whole days, when geographic distances where involved, to transact ordinary business affairs. You need only compare that with today, when transactions and other social activities are conducted globally in nano-seconds.

And there in lies one of the numerous reasons for this socio-economic chasm between then and now. This exponential increase in computational and communicative powers means countless personal identities can be stolen and exploited within incredibly short bursts of time and stretching unhindered across the planet. How can this not present a powerful incentive to those individuals or organizations so inclined. But more than that, I would venture to say that this is even far sinister than your common variety cyber-theft or digital burglary.

So what else happened between 1981 and 2018, to put so many people at such financial and personal risk? Obviously, the causes are many and somewhat convoluted. But considering the concept of the "Big Brother" t-shirt in context to what is occurring today can hopefully act as a guide post. Or even perhaps, one could equate it to a thermometer indicating that the pots about to boil and one should prepare to jump for relative safety.

In any case, the main objective is simply to connect some seemingly random planes of action that have transpired or are about to. Thereby, possibly inspiring others to look at things from a less obtuse or obstructed vantage point. Let's say, a parallax view that suddenly exposes a more true view of the approaching horizon.

*　*　*　*　*

"WWIII," The Painting Prophetic.

First off, in light of what is happening today on a global scale, I believe that one could seriously argue that WW3 has already begun to inexorably unravel into a catastrophic calamity of biblical proportions. However, due to a number of circumstances which will be elaborated shortly, the seeds of WW3 are being sowed in a tragic series of proxy wars being waged with global ramifications.

To begin with it is necessary to understand that it is of the utmost imperative that WW3 continue to be conducted as a series of unrelated proxy "theaters of war." The overriding motive stems from the fact that the powerful technologies that exists today are so advanced that it could enable a global world war to rapidly escalate into a conflagration that is so savage in destruction of property and annihilation of life that those currently in power cannot determine the ultimate outcome.

This inability to virtually guarantee a profitable outcome means those in power will lack the confidence to declare open hostilities on other superpower nation states. By keeping all conflicts localized and therefore manageable, the warfare is perceived to be more like a devastating weather disaster. Where fortunes are guaranteed from the limited death and destruction.

Today's "hybrid warfare" is always conducted by tactical operations that are designed for fairly limited geographical zones of engagement and under the elusive guise of "plausible deniability." The latter being the most crucial aspect of the limited aggression because it avoids the ramifications of proven culpability. Which would mean that the nation-state would be recognized as a warmonger and thus treated accordingly.

Hybrid warfare allows the "authorities of war" to not only maintain their "status quo" power matrix, but also extract vast fortunes of war profit from the limited, but numerous acts of military aggression. To offer credence to the claim that WW3 has already begun, let us consider the actions that are presently being aggressively engaged. While the following is fairly comprehensive, the descriptions will be brief, because what is important here is the scope and breath of activities occurring simultaneously. Also and pertaining especially to the digital battlefield, weaponry, tactics and skill sets are changing so rapidly that it is beyond the scope of this book to fully elaborate on each and every capability being presently utilized.

<u>*The Seven Deadly Signs Of World War 3*</u>

1.) Cyberwarfare and the Digital Battlefield:
     While acts of cyber-aggression are carried out across all strata of the socio-economic spectrum. What is of principal concern are the acts of cyberwarfare currently conducted on a global and daily basis. And while it may not directly result in mass casualties. Cyberwarfare can affect the infrastructure of dueling nations or states to effect vulnerabilities that can be cause for a cascading of calamitous events.
     With that in mind, consider just some of the activities that can be utilized to implement it's digital platform tactics and strategies.
     But make no mistake about it, all of the acts are willful and determined to cause harm to the enemy. The arsenal for this digital battlefield is highly dynamic and fluid. The mix of digital weaponry and tactics have yet to be fully realized and implemented.
A.) Identity Theft
     This is not your run-of-the-mill identify theft, this where millions of identities are stolen and used to reek havoc on the enemy's economic system. And one of the key components to acquire is an individuals social security number. Which when added to a few other key ingredients like credit card and debit card numbers create a potent mix of larceny.
B.) The Deep Dark Web of Illicit Black Markets
C.) Social Media & Fake News (Media Misinformation)
D.) Infrastructure Sabotage
E.) Theft of Proprietary Technology
F.) Copyright & Patent Infringement theft
G.) Malware & Ransonware
H.) Cryto-Currency & Market Manipulation

2.) The Global Military Industrial Complex
     Usually an all out declaration of war would offer the necessity for the mass manufacture of arms. But today this

industry is proliferating and profiting at record or near record levels. In addition to conventional, nuclear and cyber weaponry, there is also the advancement of military robotics or drone weaponry.

Robotics has the potential to become it's own industry by incorporating conventional and nuclear weaponry into its automation systems. Also cyber warfare will require enhanced computer components for lethal effectiveness and redundancy capability.

We were warned by the genuine honesty of an honorable American President that understood the evils of war profiteering. Being that he was probably one of the greatest military generals that the United States ever produced. But the warning, obviously, did no good.

3.) Overpopulation:

Unprecedented growth is encouraged to drive the global economic machine. Unfortunately overpopulation increases the overall and total amount of population aggression.

If it were not for the vast amounts of drugs and cheap entertainment dolled out to the masses to purposely distract and dull their capacity for comprehension. And thereby effectively pacify the population. The prison population would probably exceed the housing capacity of the ever profitable private prison industry.

4.) Proxy War's Refugees And Collateral Damage

Vast numbers of people are dying or turned refugee because they are the casualties of today's proxy micro-wars. Syrian War, terrorist attacks and drone wars. According to Wikipedia, over sixty-five million individuals have been forced to leave behind their livelihoods, family, friends and most of their earthly possessions this past year.

Obviously as a share of the vast and burgeoning global population it's but a small percentage. But really, does this in anyway actually diminish the humiliation, grief and anxiety of any one individual. We seem to act collectively as if it does. But that is a fallacy borne of our rampant hypocrisy.

5.) The sex trade and child exploitation
This unfolding tragedy is akin to the kind of devastation that would be heaped upon any conquered people as in "woe to the vanquished." These are not my "alternative" facts. They were provided by "Equality Now," an organization dedicated to a "just world for women and girls."
Trafficking women and children for sexual exploitation is the fastest growing criminal enterprise in the world. Currently it is a 100 billion dollar industry! And yet, international law and the laws of 158 countries have criminalized most of the insidious forms of trafficking.
•At least 20.9 million adults and children are bought and sold worldwide into commercial sexual servitude, forced labor and bonded labor.
•About 2 million children are exploited every year in the global commercial sex trade.
•54% of trafficking victims are trafficked for sexual exploitation.
•Women and girls make up 96% of victims of trafficking for sexual exploitation.

6.) Increased Species Extinctions Due to Man
Animals and plants, the other inhabitants of earth are becoming extinct at record rates because of extreme changes in global climatic conditions and other disruptions to the unique eco-systems of the world.
The Earth's climate is being rapidly altered as though a world war was happening. According to a recent article* published in Science magazine, the current rate of animal extinctions are a thousand times higher than without man's intervention.
*https://news.nationalgeographic.com/news/2014/05/14052 9-conservation-science-animals-species-endangered-extinctio n/

7.) The ever growing Police State:

And of course, we can't overlook the eight hundred pound Gorilla in the room or the ever growing police state, which when coupled with the private prison industry will create a modern, high tech gulag of global proportions.

Take for example the New Year's Eve celebrations in Times Square this past year. The overwhelming police presence is intended to make the public feel safe and secure. But are they really safe if they require that many police to protect them. Plus, who really pays for all this added security? And in what costs to society?

* * * * *

What Will Bring Tomorrow?

The Cold War resulted from a real power vacuum that formed in the aftermath of the complete destruction of global fascism. This power vacuum was subsequently filled by the opposing vortices of the two remaining economic and political ideologies; communism and capitalism.

World War Three will be powered by the theological discrepancies separating the three biblically based belief systems. The fact that these three religious power bases are independently mono-theist can act as a catalyst for horrific death and destruction. Either of the three are compelled to act accordingly by what is evidenced as their sacred God-given purpose of being. Simply put, anyone who stands against them must therefore stand against God.

But while they may be driven by the words of their prophet, there will be others who are driven solely by profit. Capitalism intensifies these theological flames, like fuel to a fire. As it provides a powerful profit incentive for waging destructive wars. And thus offers the "Godless" war profiteer plenty of opportunities to extract obscene fortunes from the carnal wastelands of raging battlefields or military playgrounds.

And then there is the catalyst that I've termed the "Devil's Brew." While petroleum is basically another of Earth's planetary resources and inherently benign. When this ancient substance is mixed with modern greed it becomes a highly deadly concoction that is not only lethal to all of earth's inhabitants but incredibly corrosive to man's soul. An evil brew that the devil drinks everyday with an unquenchable thirst.

What more can I say? Other than it would appear by what I've written, that to free us from our chains of tyrannical greed, it will first be necessary to enlighten ourselves enough to truly unite and act to stop the mania of conspicuous materialism and selling our souls for greedy gain.

Until then may God have mercy on our souls, because the devil will have his day and so the innocent good thus pay.

Chapter Nine:

A Look Back To The Future.

This is a reproduction of the original ad from "Rolling Stone" magazine dated Nov. 1981.

By chance, the "Big Brother" t-shirt ad was placed opposite of the John Lennon ad in "Rolling Stone" magazine.

Serendipitous optical aberration creates visual illusion of "Death Ray" shooting from the right eye of the beast. (Sun Valley Studios 1981) Photo credit/Thomas Favelli

Artist and author painting in the flames of WWIII with real fire. (Sun Valley Studios 1981) Photo credit/Thomas Favelli